Sacred
Poems
and
Prayers
of Love

Chosen and Introduced

by

Mary Ford-Grabowsky

DOUBLEDAY
New York • London • Toronto • Sydney • Auckland

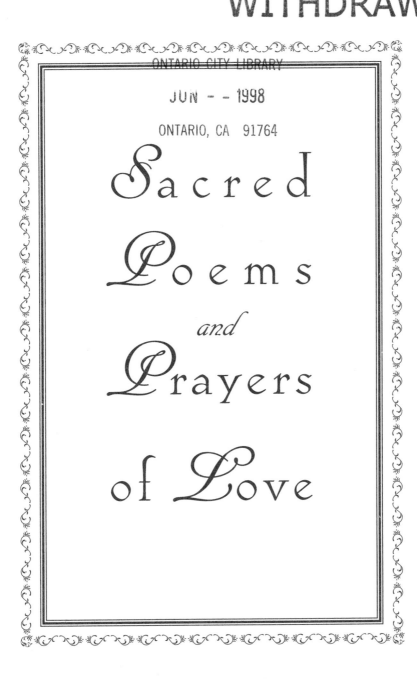

Sacred Poems

and

Prayers

of Love

To Andrew Harvey and Eryk Hanut

PUBLISHED BY DOUBLEDAY
a division of Bantam Doubleday Dell Publishing Group, Inc.
1540 Broadway, New York, New York 10036

DOUBLEDAY and the portrayal of an anchor with a dolphin are trademarks
of Doubleday, a division of Bantam Doubleday Dell Publishing Group, Inc.

Book design by Julie Duquet

Library of Congress Cataloging-in-Publication Data
Sacred poems and prayers of love / chosen and introduced
by Mary Ford-Grabowsky.
p.   cm.
Includes index.
1. Love—Poetry.   2. Prayers.   I. Ford-Grabowsky, Mary.
PN6110.L6S25   1998
808.81—dc21   97-25051
CIP

ISBN 0-385-48702-9
Copyright © 1998 by Mary Ford-Grabowsky

Printed in the United States of America
February 1998

1   3   5   7   9   10   8   6   4   2
First Edition

Contents

Introduction

Prayers of Love

The world's most beautiful prayers speak about love and blaze with love. African, American, from the Far East, Australia or India, prayers about love celebrate the many ways in which men and women experience the simple, sublime, and profoundly beautiful sense of connectedness to God, one another, and the world that we name "love." In *Sacred Poems and Prayers of Love,* there are psalms and hymns, sacred poems and songs of praise from the world's vast treasury of spiritual writings honoring the nobility and dignity of the human spirit that comes into being when we love. Love is presented as life's greatest and most intangible gift and blessing; as the source of awe and consolation and happiness; as the origin of bliss and of feelings of gratitude and forgiveness; as the ecstasy of uniting with the beloved; as the ultimate origin, meaning, direction, and purpose of all life and all creation.

Every entry in *Sacred Poems and Prayers of Love* has been chosen for its wealth of feeling, poetry, spiritual radiance, and power. In place of the solemn, alienating prayers so often transmitted in the West in the past four hundred years, this book offers only gorgeous, evocative, comforting, healing, strengthening language for the soul.

Whereas the spirituality informing this book is pre-modern—close to the earth's green fields and starlit skies—the book has been created for post-modern people: men and women attuned to science, technology, and the internet, who long ago lost interest in superficial, irrelevant, naive, or sentimental prayers. *Sacred Poems and Prayers of Love* mines the deeper, more ancient layers of the earth for sensitive and artistic works, some familiar and some unknown, but all vibrantly alive in the love that illumines the human heart and makes life a holy mystery.

The Many Forms of Love

The selections in this book have been arranged in eight chapters according to the major kinds of love: love for life and the beauty of the earth; romantic love; friendship; love for family members; love of neighbor (compassion for all people); loving in times of suffering; mystical love; and Divine love in everyone and everything.

Some prayers come from the mystical streams of the world's five great religions: Christianity, Judaism, Islam, Hinduism, and Buddhism. Others originate in smaller faiths like Jainism and Baha'ism. Still others belong to spiritual traditions such as the Celtic, Aztec, or Native American. Written or transmitted orally, representing some thirty centuries of human history, the poems and prayers in this collection exemplify the heights and depths of love refined and uplifted by grace to the level of the Divine.

The prayers in this book record every ecstasy of the spirit—and every agony—that relatedness entails. Revealing a universal pattern of longing, fulfillment, loss, and grief that leads to a final vision of oneness with the beloved, these poems and prayers recount the many aspects of love encountered along the spiritual path. Some tell the story of travelers who stand at the base of the holy mountainside, yearning, like Dante, to mount from love of neighbor as oneself to love of God. Others, like Sadhu Sundar Singh's, note the slow progress of lovers circling around and around the mountain longing for oneness with the true, the good, and the beautiful. Still others, like Thomas Renaud's powerful "Day of the Lion," describe the harder realities of the spiritual life. Writings of Rumi, Rabia, Kabir, and Mirabai are included to convey the radical joy of those who catch sight of the holy heights and fall to their knees, rapt in the vision of "That Which Is."

Although the past holds a prominent place in this book, some of the book's loveliest prayers issue from the waning years of the twentieth century. A number were written specifically for this collection by spiritual leaders, prominent scholars, mystics, and contemplatives; among them are Brother David Steindl-Rast, Mother Tessa Bielecki, Andrew Harvey, Eryk Hanut, and Sri Eknath Easwaran. "The Course of Mystical Love," composed by Brother Wayne Teasdale, a leader in interfaith work, stems from the contemporary rediscovery of the world's mystical traditions. Jeremy Taylor's eloquent prayer for ever deeper love reflects a central struggle in the spiritual life today. Several prayers mark the twentieth century's last-minute recovery of ecological love, so disastrously lost during the earlier years of the scientific age. Margaret Payne's moving poem celebrates the current emergence of urban spirituality, and Mel Bricker's "Canticle" signals our reawakening to the sacredness of the body.

The poems and prayers in this collection come from dissimilar times and places around the globe, from people who differ widely in many ways and yet are one in the sacred knowledge that love is a gift, a most precious and sacred gift, to be welcomed and given at every moment with all one's heart. Lyrics of love inspire us to receive existence gratefully from the Fountain of Life, and strive to leave for our children and for all generations to come a memory of our love.

The Sacredness of Love

The holy energy that fills the world, driving crashing waves along golden sands, sending gentle breezes over rippling ponds, pouring warmth and moisture over hardened earth in the spring, evokes in the human soul an awareness of everlasting order deep within and beyond the seemingly futile centuries of history. Bright and beautiful, holy with hope and the power to love, this Blessed One, the Tao, the Infinite, brings undying assurance that all creation is welcomed to life, invited as to a sacred meal. Deep calls unto deep forever, as Saint Paul said. Life echoes eternally a call and a beckoning to love and be loved. At the first there was love. Love will be at the last. Love is truth, reality, beauty, the final meaning and secret of existence.

From all eternity and for all time, the breath of love, like a quiet whisper in the night, brushes softly over the beings of the earth— announcing unnameable mysteries, ineffable depths. Whoever receives the exquisite currents willingly breaks open and grows beautiful, like a flower in spring. Whoever surrenders to these holy inevitabilities will see in their own deep relationship with Reality, as in a mirror of God's enormity, the shimmering light that gives all of life its golden sheen.

Rainer Maria Rilke, in a state of rapture, once prayed: "Don't you sense me, ready to break into being at your touch?" As love multiplied to infinities in his soul, as he felt the approach of the inner self made of white light and grounded in translucency, he embraced a life full of grace, summed up in love. With the adoration accorded to a beloved, Rilke listened to what he heard in the air all around him and responded to "the gigantic call" with magnificent words. Faced with a truth too holy for expression, he transformed simple words into beautiful symbols of the Absolute:

> Voices. Voices. Listen my heart, as
>   only
> saints have listened: until the gigantic
>   call lifted them
> off the ground; yet they kept on,
>   impossibly,
> kneeling and didn't notice at all:
> so complete was their listening. Not
>   that you could endure
> God's voice—far from it. But listen to
>   the voice of the wind
> and the ceaseless message that forms
>   itself out of silence.

Like all illumined people, Rilke was caught up in a pure, direct, Divine experience of love that enabled him to shout with joy and to clothe even the deepest grief in jewels. Inconceivable, incomparable, unnameable, unutterable, this love—the love from which all has come to be, through which all endures—calls us by name to the grand adventure of creation, asking each of us to return in love to the endlessly loving One.

Chapter 1

Love

for

Life

and the

Beauty

of the

Earth

"We are in the world to love the world," a poet wrote: the whole wild variety of flowers, fruits, foods, leaves, and trees. We are in the world to love the nobility of a forest, the dignity of a big animal, and seas that "press madly upon the land." We are in the world to love dawn rolling over the hills with golden light, and dusk closing a day with dark light worthy of reverence.

We are here to be moved by the sounds of the world, the sacred reverberations rising and falling throughout the universe, inviting us to celebrate and sing, to dance with our raptures and ecstasies, to ponder sounds audible only in prayer. We are in the world to care lovingly for the ill and lonely and elderly; to touch joyfully soft fabrics, warm grasses, and massive rocks. We are here to know through our bodies and hands and minds that all things exist in and through and for the Holy One that is Love Itself. We are put on earth, as William Blake observed, to learn to bear the beams of love.

In a beautiful mystical passage, the author Vera Brittain speaks of a friend's awakening spiritually to the full implications of loving life, of living in the present moment, of becoming one's fullest self, of discovering meaning and depth in the smallest event. She describes her friend's experience this way:

At the age of 33, while at the height of her power as a novelist, Winifred Holtby was told she might not have more than two years to live. [Despairing and exhausted,] her whole being in rebellion, she was walking up a hill and came to a trough outside a farm-house. Its surface was frozen over and some lambs were gathered around it.

She broke the ice for the lambs with her stick, and as she did so heard a voice within her saying, 'Having nothing, yet possessing all things.'

It was so distinct that she looked around startled, but she was alone with the lambs on the top of the hill. Suddenly in a flash, the grief, the bitterness, the sense of frustration disappeared; all desire to possess power and glory for herself vanished away, and never came back.

She later associated her moment of transformation on the hill with the saying: "And now we are saved absolutely; we need not say from what; we are at home in the universe."

Releasing the thirsty lambs from their helpless suffering, Winifred Holtby transcended her own radical suffering and became "at home in the universe." Plunging deep roots into the fruitful soil of the earth, she felt for the first time in her life that she belonged, that she was connected to living beings, one with the lambs and water and ice and sticks and sky, attached and redeemed and made whole. Her spirit freed, like the water under the heavy layer of ice, she became one with creation and with herself, her body no longer detached, the Divine spark at the center of her soul at last in flames.

To fall in love with life, and remain in love with life, to have the fullest possible experience of the beauty of creation, and of the Divine in everything, the little spark at our innermost center must be lit and tended and kept alive. As a Jewish mystic wrote, "A person is like a bed of coals." The flame may burn low, detaching us from the beautiful beings of the world, but as long as a single spark is left, the fire can be kindled once more.

Inscribed on a Temple

I face the distant peaks of Chin,
Country blue and still after rain,
Trees merging into far twilight,
Smells of grass blown into my cave,
Who would want a life beyond this?
Here, around us, endless beauty.
Now, around us, endless wonder.

Han Hung: China, eighth century

Stay Up Till Dawn

Some nights, stay up till dawn,
As the moon sometimes does for the sun.
Be a full bucket pulled up the dark way
of a well, then lifted out into light.

Something opens our wings. Something
makes boredom and hurt disappear.
Someone fills the cup in front of us.
We taste only sacredness.

Source unknown

In the Beginning Was the Gift

In the beginning was the gift.
And the gift was with God and the gift was God.
And the gift came and set its tent among us,
first in the form of a fireball
that burned unabated for 750,000 years
and cooked in its immensely hot oven
hadrons and leptons.
These gifts found a modicum of stability,
enough to give birth to the first atomic creatures,
hydrogen and helium.
A billion years of stewing and stirring
and the gifts of hydrogen and helium
birthed galaxies—spinning, whirling, alive galaxies
created trillions of stars,
lights in the heavens and cosmic furnaces
that made more gifts
through violent explosions of vast supernovas
burning abright with the glow
of more than a billion stars.
Gifts upon gifts, gifts birthing gifts, gifts exploding,
gifts imploding, gifts of light, gifts of darkness.
Cosmic gifts and subatomic gifts.
All drifting and swirling, being born and dying,
in some vast secret of a plan.
Which was also a gift.
One of these supernova gifts exploded in a special manner
sending a unique gift to the universe,
which later-coming creatures would one day call

earth,
their home.
Its biosphere was also a gift,
wrapping it with beauty and dignity and just the right
protection from sun's radiation
and from the cosmic cold.
And eternal night.
This gifted planet was set as a jewel
in its most exquisite setting,
in this case, the exact distance of 100 million miles
from its mother star, the sun.
New gifts arose, never seen in such forms in the universe—
rocks, oceans, continents,
multicellular creatures that moved by their own inner power.
Life was born!
Gifts that had taken the form of fireball and helium,
galaxies and stars, rock and water, now took the form of Life!
Life—a new gift of the universe, a new gift in the universe.
Flowers of multiple color and scent, trees standing upright.
Forests arose offering places for all manner
of creeping, crawling things.
Of things that fly and sing.
Of things that swim and slither.
Of things that run on four legs.
And, eventually,
of things that stand and walk on two.
With thumbs that move to make still more creativity—
more gift making—
possible.

The human became a gift, but also a menace.
For its powers of creativity were unique in their potential
for destruction or healing.
How would humans use these gifts?
Which direction would they choose?
The earth waited for an answer to these questions.
And is still waiting. . . .

Matthew Fox; United States, twentieth century

Springtime that was: the great world was receiving spring weather, and the east winds moderated their wintry blast. Then it was that the first cattle drank in the light and humanity's iron race reared its head from the harsh fields, and wild beasts were let loose into the forests and the stars into heaven. And tender things could not have endured this world's stress without such long pause between the season's cold and heat, and without heaven's gracious welcome to the newborn earth.

Vergil, Rome, 70 B.C.–19 B.C.

Prayer When Opening a Door

Prayer when opening a door:
I pray you, Lord, to open the door of my heart to receive you
  within my heart.
When washing clothes:
I pray you, Lord, to wash my heart, making me white as snow.
When sweeping floors:
I pray you, Lord, to sweep away my heart's uncleanness, that my
  heart may always be pure.
When pouring oil:
I pray you, Lord, to give me wisdom like the wise virgins who
  always had oil in their vessels.
When posting a letter:
I pray you, Lord, to add to me faith upon faith, that I may always
  have communication with you.
When lighting lamps:
I pray you, Lord, to make my deeds excellent like lamps before
  others, and more, to place your true light within my heart.
When watering flowers:
I pray you, Lord, to send down spiritual rain into my heart, to
  germinate the good seed there.
When boiling water for tea:
I pray you, Lord, to send down spiritual fire to burn away the
  coldness of my heart and that I may always be hot-hearted in
  serving you.

Anonymous, China

Praise Be to You, Our Creator:
Inspired by St. Francis of Assisi

Glorious Creator, source of all that is, to you our highest praise and glory and honor and blessing.

Praise be to you, our Creator, for Father Sun, who gives us light and warmth and life. His coming forth and his going away shape the rhythms of our world, our seasons, our lives.

Praise be to you, our Creator, for Mother Earth, who gives us daily our bodies, our sustenance, our home. Her generosity and her nurturing are endless. May we learn to treat her with the loving thanks that she deserves.

Praise be to you, our Creator, for Brother Wind, our very breath, and for the freshness and change he brings with his coming.

Praise be you, our Creator, for Sister Water, so bountiful and yet so precious, who washes us and sustains us and caresses us with love.

Praise be to you, our Creator, for Brother Fire, in whose hunger and brightness and reaching and power we see an image of our own. May we learn to treat our fires with the care we have learned for his.

Praise be to you, our Creator, for our Selves. In the spirit and energy and creativity and diversity you give each of us we are tiny mirrors of your own Spirit and Energy and Creativity and Diversity, and of all that you have made. May we remember your divinity, and ours, and that of all that you have made, as we live our lives in your wondrous Creation.

Jon Martin Schwartz; United States, twentieth century

Thou Art the Sky

Thou art the sky and Thou art the nest as well.
O Thou beautiful, there in the nest it is Thy love that encloses the
  soul with colours and sounds and odours.
There comes the morning with the golden basket in her right hand
  bearing the wreath of beauty, silently to crown the earth.
And there comes the evening over the lonely meadow deserted by
  herds, through trackless paths, carrying cool draughts of peace in
  her golden pitcher from the western ocean of rest.
But there, where spreads the infinite sky for the soul to take her
  flight in, reigns the stainless white radiance, there is no day nor
  night, nor form nor colour, and never, never a word.

Rabindranath Tagore; India, 1861-1941

Blessed be you, harsh matter, barren soil, stubborn rock: you who yield only to violence, you who force us to work if we would eat. Blessed be you, perilous matter, violent sea, untameable passion: you who unless we fetter you will devour us. Blessed be you, mighty matter, irresistible march of evolution, reality ever new-born; you who, by constantly shattering our mental categories, force us to go ever further and further in our pursuit of the truth. Blessed be you, universal matter, unmeasurable time, boundless ether, triple abyss of stars and atoms and generations; you who by overflowing and dissolving our narrow standards of measurement reveal to us the dimensions of God. . . .

Teilhard de Chardin; France, 1881-1955

CANTICLE

I praise you for laughing eyes splashing joy in somber places
working love over open hearts.

I praise you for bodies striding, stretching, walking,
    running,
stooped, long-limbed, glistening, wrinkled, soaking on air,
alive to sunlight and the balm of evening shadows.

I praise you for water wonders roaring around one's feet,
inundating, surrounding, lifting, working, quenching,
    surging,
and dropping gently on joy, on hummingbirds, and
    children's
noses—and inviting our souls to vibrant reverence.

Mel Bricker; United States, twentieth century

The Moon of Love Is Rising Full

Sing, O bird that nestles deep within my heart!
Sing, O bird, that sits on the Kalpa-Tree of Brahman!
Sing God's everlasting praise . . .

Then he sang:

Brahman, Joy of the whole universe, Supreme effulgence;
God beginningless, Lord of the world, the very Life of life! . . .

And again:

O King of Kings, reveal Yourself to me!
I crave Your mercy. Cast on me Your glance!
At Your feet I dedicate my life,
Sacred in the fiery furnace of this world. . . .

Upon the tray of the sky blaze bright
The lamps of sun and moon;
Like diamonds shine the glittering stars
To deck Your wondrous form;
The sweet Malaya breeze blows soft,
For fragrant incense smoke;
The moving air sways to and fro
The fan before Your holy face;
Like gleaming votive lights the fresh and flowery groves appear.
How wonderful Your worship is! . . .

He sang again:

In Wisdom's firmament the moon of love is rising full.
And Love's flood-tide, in surging waves, is flowing everywhere.
O Lord, how full of bliss You are!

Ramakrishna; India, 1836-1886

Shall I abandon, O King of Mysteries, the soft
comforts of home? Shall I turn my back on
my native land, and my face towards the sea?

Shall I put myself wholly at the mercy of God,
without silver, without a horse, without fame
and honour? Shall I throw myself wholly on
the King of kings, without sword and shield,
without food and drink, without a bed to lie
on?

Shall I say farewell to my beautiful land,
placing myself under Christ's yoke? Shall I pour
out my heart to him, confessing my manifold
sins and begging forgiveness, tears streaming
down my cheeks?

Shall I leave the prints of my knees on the
sandy beach, a record of my final prayer in
my native land? Shall I then suffer every kind
of wound that the sea can inflict?

Shall I take my tiny coracle across the wide,
sparkling ocean? O King of the Glorious
Heaven, shall I go of my own choice upon
the sea?

O Christ, will you help me on the wild waves?

Celtic oral tradition; Scotland, Wales,
England, Ireland, first millennium

I see You in all things, O my God. Infinity itself is Your creation. And all around are the signs of Your endlessness: the bursting life of countless plants; the unending song of innumerable birds; the tireless movement of animals and insects. Nowhere can I see a beginning or an end. I see infinite beauty infuse your entire world . . .

The sun is Your eye during the day, and the moon is Your eye at night. The wind is Your breath, and the fertile earth is Your heart . . .

As the waters of a river flow to the sea, the path determined by the line of the valley, so we pass through life to death, our destiny mapped out by Your will.

Arjuna; India, c. eighth century B. C.

Hymn to the Creator

The earth is full of your goodness,
your greatness and understanding,
your wisdom and harmony.
How wonderful
are the lights that you created.
You formed them
with strength and power
and they shine very wonderfully on the world,
magnificent in their splendour.
They arise in radiance
and go down in joy.
Reverently
they fulfill your divine will.
They are tributes to your name
as they exalt your sovereign rule
in song.

*Jewish mystical hymn; from the time of the Second
Temple, c. 516 B.C.-70 A.D.*

The Sacred Berry

Hold a ripe strawberry, green crown intact.

Oh sweet gift to the Seneca, I admire you. You are shaped like the
heart to remind us that we are to live by the heart.
Your flesh is red, to tell us our hearts should be moist with blood,
never dry and brown and crackly.
We study the seeds on the outside. They are many, to teach us that
there are many ways in the world to believe, to understand life.
All are worthy of respect.
We finger the leaves, so we keep in mind that we must always stay
connected to Mother Earth and appreciate her gifts.
Now, we eat this beautiful strawberry from the bottom up (in
silence), relishing the sweet taste. For the last bite we eat berry
and leaf together to help us remember life holds bitter tastes with
sweet. For all, we keep a thankful heart.

Seneca oral tradition; Native America
Recorded by José Hobday

EVERY CREATURE IS A BOOK ABOUT GOD

Apprehend God in all things,
For God is in all things.
Every single creature is full of God
And is a book about God.
Every creature is a word of God.

If I spent enough time with the tiniest creature—
Even a caterpillar—
I would never have to prepare a sermon.
So full of God
Is every being.

Meister Eckhart, Germany, c. 1260–1327

THE MOTOR UNDER ME IS RUNNING HOT

Lord,
the motor under me is running hot.
Lord, there are twenty-eight people
and lots of luggage in the truck.
Underneath are my bad tires.
The brakes are unreliable.
Unfortunately I have no money,
and parts are difficult to get.
Lord,
I did not overload the truck.
Lord, "Jesus is mine"
is written on the vehicle,
for without him I would not drive a single mile.
The people in the back are relying on me.
They trust me because they see the words:
"Jesus is mine."
Lord,
I trust you!
First comes the straight road
with little danger,
I can keep my eyes on the women,
children and chickens in the village.
But soon the road begins to turn,
it goes up and down,
it jumps and dances,
this death-road to Kumasi.
Tractors carrying mahogany trunks drive
as if there were no right or left.

Lord,
Kumasi is the temptation
to take more people than we should.
Let's overcome it!
The road to Accra is another problem.
Truck drivers try to beat the record,
although the road is poor
and has many holes
and there are many curves
before we come to the hills.
And finally to Akwasim.
Passing large churches in every village,
I am reminded of you, and in reverence
I take off my hat.
Now downhill in second gear.

Anonymous; Ghana, twentieth century

FROM *Holy the Firm*

Every day is a god, each day is a god, and holiness holds forth in
   time. I worship each god, I praise each day splintered down,
   splintered down and wrapped in time like a husk, a husk of many
   colors spreading, at dawn fast over the mountain's split.
I wake in a god. I wake in arms holding my quilt, holding me as
   best they can inside my quilt.
Someone is kissing me—already. I wake, I cry "Oh," I rise from
   the pillow. Why should I open my eyes?
I open my eyes. The god lifts from the water. His head fills the
   bay. He is Puget Sound, the Pacific, his breast rises from
   pastures, his fingers are firs, islands slide wet down his shoulders.
   Islands slip blue from his shoulders and glide over the water, the
   empty, lighted water like a stage.
Today's god rises, his long eyes flecked in clouds. He flings his
   arms, spreading colors, he arches, cupping sky in his belly, he
   vaults, vaulting and spread, holding all the spread on me like
   skin.

Annie Dillard, United States, twentieth century

I Hear Him Coming

The Sun, the Light of the world,
I hear Him coming.
I see His face as He comes.
He makes the beings on earth happy,
And they rejoice.
O Wakan-Tanka, I offer to You this world of Light.

Kablaya of the Oglala Sioux; Native America, traditional

THE WAY OF THE THREE STEPS:
A NATIVE AMERICAN PRAYER TO BEGIN THE DAY

STAND ON MOTHER EARTH. FACE ANY DIRECTION YOU CHOOSE.
(TAKE ONE STEP FORWARD, AS YOU LOOK ABOUT, UP AND DOWN:)

O Great, Holy Spirit, I take this step into the *day* you have given.
I embrace all I see—the season, the wind, the fragrances, the
weather. Let me always accept the day given with a grateful
heart.

(TAKE ANOTHER STEP FORWARD.)

O Spirit of Life, I put my arms around *myself*, all that I am, all
that I can be. I stand here in my own history, with all my
mistakes and victories. I hold all those I will meet today, in my
journeying and in my work. I try to walk gently on this earth.
Let me walk gently through the lives of my work companions
and friends. Though they make way for my passing, may they
spring back, neither broken nor bruised.

(TAKE ANOTHER STEP FORWARD.)

Oh glorious Spirit of *mystery*, I put my arms around you. I do not
know what will happen to me today, but I accept it. Give me a
heart of courage and believing, so I may put my trust in you,
and fear nothing.

From the Plains tribes; Native America
Recorded by José Hobday

I Arise Today

I arise today
Through a mighty strength:
    God's power to guide me,
    God's might to uphold me,
    God's wisdom to teach me,
    God's eyes to watch over me;
    God's ear to hear me,
    God's word to give me speech,
    God's hand to guard me,
    God's way to lie before me,
    God's shield to shelter me,
    God's host to secure me.

Bridgid of Gael; Ireland,
first millennium

O Burning Mountain

O burning mountain, O chosen sun,
O perfect moon, O fathomless well,
O unattainable height, O clearness beyond measure,
O wisdom without end, O mercy without limit,
O strength beyond resistance, O crown of all majesty,
The humblest you created sings your praise.

Mechthild of Magdeburg; Germany, c. 1212–c. 1280

WE RETURN THANKS

We return thanks to our mother, the earth, which sustains us. We
   return thanks to the rivers and streams, which supply us with
   water. We return thanks to all herbs, which furnish medicines for
   the cure of our diseases. We return thanks to the corn, and to
   her sisters, the beans and squashes, which give us life. We return
   thanks to the bushes and trees, which provide us with fruit. We
   return thanks to the wind, which, moving the air, has banished
   diseases. We return thanks to the moon and stars, which have
   given us their light when the sun was gone. We return thanks to
   our grandfather He-no, that he has protected his grandchildren
   from witches and reptiles, and has given us his rain. We return
   thanks to the sun, that he has looked upon the earth with a
   beneficent eye. Lastly, we return thanks to the Great Spirit, in
   whom is embodied all goodness, and who directs all things for
   the good of his children.

Iroquois oral tradition; Native America

A Bahá'í Prayer

Blessed is the spot, and the house, and the place,
and the city, and the heart, and the mountain,
and the refuge, and the cave, and the valley, and
the land, and the sea, and the island, and the
meadow where mention of God has been made,
and His praise glorified.

Bahá'u'lláh; Iran, 1817-1892

A Sufi Prayer

Know the world from end to end is a mirror;
In each atom a hundred stars are concealed.
If you pierce the heart of a single drop of water,
From it will flow a hundred dear oceans;
If you look intently at each speck of dust,
In it you will see a thousand beings;
A gnat in its lines is like an elephant;
In name a drop of water resembles the Nile,
In the heart of a barley-corn is stored a hundred harvests,
Within a millet-seed a world exists.
In an insect's wing is an ocean of life,
A heaven is concealed in the pupil of an eye,
The core in the centre of the heart is small,
Yet the Lord of both worlds will enter there.

Mahmud ash-Shabistari; Persia, c. 1250-c. 1320

THE SEVEN DIRECTIONS

(STAND ON MOTHER EARTH. FACE EAST.)

Oh Great Spirit of the East, I face you to understand birth and
new beginnings. I look to you bringing forth a new day and am
reminded that life is about birth—of babies, puppies, new
seasons, new ways of doing things. Teach me the mysteries of
Beginnings.

(FACE SOUTH.)

Oh Great Spirit of the South, I look to you to understand
abundance, fertility, warmth and the extravagance and colors of
creation. Come to my mind and feet and lead me into the
adventures of the South.

(FACE WEST.)

Oh Spirit of the West, I turn to you to understand dying. As the
sun goes down each day, I am reminded of many deaths: friends,
generations, the seasons, and old ways of doing things. Let the
sunset remind me that, like the sun, I too shall arise in a new
life and color.

(FACE NORTH.)

Oh Strong, Powerful North, I face you to remember that life
sometimes comes to us in cold and harshness. Not only do the

days grow cold, but others may turn cold toward us. Give me the strength of the Buffalo, that I may stand in the blizzards with my face toward the North, without being blown down or overwhelmed.

(FACE EAST AGAIN. LOOK UP.)

Oh Great Spirit of all that is *Up*, all that soars, all that floats or flies above us, all that comes to us from on high to enlighten us, I cherish this direction. Give me visions, and let my mind walk among the stars and moon, and in the daylight of the Sun. Oh Sweet power of UP, lift me high to my Father, the Sky.

(STILL FACING EAST. LOOK DOWN.)

Oh Great Spirit of all that is *Down*, I thank you for my Mother, the Earth. I ask to be humble, to be simple, to never consider myself above all my relatives of creation. And may I walk with such respect upon the earth, that when it is time for me to go to her, she may receive me sweetly to her heart.

(STILL FACING EAST.)

Oh Wondrous Direction of *In*, I put my hand on my heart to remind me of the mysteries, the unknowns that lie within me. Teach me to guard the simpler beauties, to walk closely within the circle of my

God in my heart. Let me share only with those who can be loyal to my secrets.

Ho! So it is! . . .

Iroquois oral tradition; Native America
Recorded by José Hobday

The content of this prayer will vary every day and with every person. Only the form is given.

PRAISE

Infinite Source of All Creation:
I praise you for sparkling rivers
that dance with the light.

I praise you for mystical lakes
ringed by mountains and mist.

I praise you for small creatures,
for my cat who would share one breath with me.

I praise you for butterflies,
and dragonflies,
and wasps who mind their own business.

I praise you for frogs and toads
and turtles and for
lizards, large and small.

I praise you for fertile soil,
and clean water,
and for mud between my toes.

I praise you for rabbits and bears and whales
and owls and wolves and foxes
—all wearing white—
and for the crunch of packed powder snow
    beneath my feet
in the moonlight.

I praise you for all the winged ones
but especially for pelicans, cormorants, and
    shovelers,
for herons and egrets,
for Chuck Will's widows and red-winged
    blackbirds,
for magpies and grackles, and for hawks and
    crows.
These mighty spirits ever lift us
in praise.

I praise you for Awe and Joy and Love,
for Surprise and Oneness.

Judy Gaar, United States, twentieth century

Columba's Rock

Delightful it is to stand on the peak of a rock,
in the bosom of the isle, gazing on the face
of the sea.

I hear the heaving waves chanting a tune to
God in heaven, I see their glittering surf

I see the golden beaches, their sands sparkling,
I hear the joyous shrieks of the swooping gulls

I hear the waves breaking, crashing on rocks,
like thunder in heaven. I see the mighty whales.

I watch the ebb and flow of the ocean tide,
it holds my secret, my mournful flight from Eire.

Contrition fills my heart as I hear the sea,
it chants my sins, sins too numerous to confess.

Let me bless almighty God, whose power extends
over sea and land, whose angels watch over all.

Let me study sacred books to calm my soul;
I pray for peace, kneeling at heaven's gates.

Let me do my daily work, gathering seaweed,
catching fish, giving food to the poor.

Let me say my daily prayers, sometimes chanting, sometimes quiet, always thanking God.

Delightful it is to live on a peaceful isle, in a quiet cell, serving the King of kings.

Celtic oral tradition; England, Ireland, Scotland, Wales, first millennium

SACRED

I'm an Indian.
I think about common things like this pot.
The bubbling water comes from the rain cloud.
It represents the sky.
The fire comes from the sun
which warms us all, men, animals, trees.
The meat stands for the four-legged creatures,
our animal brothers,
who gave of themselves so that we should live.
The steam is living breath.
It was water, now it goes up to the sky,
becomes a cloud again.
These things are sacred.
Looking at that pot full of good soup,
I am thinking how, in this simple manner,
The Great Spirit takes care of me.
John Lame Deer, Native America, twentieth century

The New Moon

The new moon, as its
name suggests, renews
itself; how marvelous
it is in this change,
a beacon to the hosts
on high, shining in the
vault of the heavens!

Sirach 43:8

A Sioux Indian Prayer

Ho! Great Spirit, Grandfather, you have made everything and are in everything. You sustain everything, guide everything, provide everything and protect everything because everything belongs to you. I am weak, poor and lowly, nevertheless help me to care in appreciation and gratitude to you and for everything. I love the stars, the sun and the moon and I thank you for our beautiful mother the earth whose many breasts nourish the fish, the fowls and the animals too. May I never deceive mother earth, may I never deceive other people, may I never deceive myself, and above all may I never deceive you.

Adapted by Bishop Vine Deloria from the Sioux oral tradition; Native America

FROM *Song of Myself:* A Meditation on Animals

I think I could turn and live with animals, they are so placid and
    self-contained;
I stand and look at them long and long.
They do not sweat and whine about their condition;
They do not lie awake in the dark and weep for their sins;
They do not make me sick discussing their duty to God;
Not one is dissatisfied—not one is demented with the mania of
    owning things;
Not one kneels to another, nor to his kind that lived thousands of
    years ago;
Not one is respectable or industrious over the whole earth.

Walt Whitman; United States, 1819-1892

MAY MY PRAYER BE BEAUTIFUL

The garden is rich with diversity
With plants of a hundred families
In the space between the trees
With all the colors and fragrances.
Basil, mint and lavender,
God keep my remembrance pure,
Raspberry, apple, rose,
God fill my heart with love,
Dill, anise, tansy,
Holy winds blow in me.
Rhododendron, zinnia,
May my prayer be beautiful
May my remembrance, O God, be as incense to you
In the sacred grove of eternity
As I smell and remember
The ancient forests of earth.

A Chinook song: Native America,
recorded c. nineteenth century

Pine needles pray,
nestling down.
Their scent rises.
The Forest breathes
and exhales prayer.
Its wind moves
into fissures.
Granite takes
it in
and firmly
issues a
prayer to
a mushroom
lifted by its
bold touch
and sends it
down to
the juicy
soil-cracked
seeds
whose prayer
makes the
Forest tingle
down into the
roots of
the Great Oak
embracing
them all

Join in
praying
now.
Take it
in.
Ingest the
prayers
of the
land.
Unutterable
language
enters our
nose
invisible
waves
open our
pores.
The senses
begin
to pray.
All that we
learned
hushed
by the
longing
of
the Forest.
The prayer

and touching   of the
the Great   primal
River of   lover
Light only   rises
those who   no longer
pray can   only
enter.   human.

Jim Roberts; United States, twentieth century

THERE ARE SUFIS EVERYWHERE

There came a gathering of Sufis this morning—
Where at dawn's first rays I saw assembled 1000 white birds
upon a lake.
Morning prayer had begun.
With complete abandon each bird cried out God's name in praise
Over and over again.
Whirling and dancing in a heavenly delight
They were filled on God's bounty.
Finally, completely surrendered, they arose as One.
Their freedom written in great sky circles as they took flight.
"Friend there is no hiding the naked beauty of the ecstatic."

Jalal al-Din Rumi, Persia, 1207-1273

CREATION

The beauty of the trees,
the softness of the air,
the fragrance of the grass,
    speak to me.

The summit of the mountain,
the thunder of the sky
the rhythm of the sea,
    speak to me.

The faintness of the stars,
the freshness of the morning,
the dewdrop in the flower,
    speak to me.

The strength of the fire,
the taste of the salmon,
the trail of the sun,
and the life that never goes away,
    they speak to me.

And my heart soars.
    Chief Dan George, Native America

Chapter 2

Falling

in

Love

The beauty of physical desire sanctifies the entire universe for those who love. Blazing with rapture and bliss, with elation and luminous joy, romantic love weaves a union that mirrors the mystic's ecstatic communion with God. "Love you? I *am* you," Charles Williams wrote to his beloved when he felt that inebriating oneness all lovers feel when barriers melt away, time suspends its flight, and we dissolve into one another like dawn into day.

Seeing the other with love's "vast gaze," as Rainer Maria Rilke wrote, lovers "stare beyond" into the radiant black velvet of eternity. Leaping over the inner wall of selfishness, pressing against the warm flesh of another, pressing into the holy horizon of love itself, lovers watch the unclothing of the beloved and disappear like mystics into a sacred night. Here in the magic of full self-forgetfulness, in the totally incomprehensible miracle of self-transcendence, in the supercharged mystery of human passion, lies the spirituality of erotic love. Eros is a divine connecting principle that makes lovers willing to sacrifice even their lives for the sake of the beloved. When eros dethrones the ego from its place of centrality in the soul, planting the interests of another where self-concern used to loom, we feel a promise of liberation, of delicious freedom and undying passion, of soaring forever in weightless flight.

The gorgeous lyrics of Mirabai, one of India's greatest mystics, celebrate love with images of wild embraces and ardent nights as sensual and voluptuous as they are spiritual. All of the longings of humankind seem to well up in her erotic poems, as in the following:

I am thirsting for your love, O my beloved,
I shall make this body a lamp, and my tender heart shall be its
wick;
I shall fill it with the scented oil of my young love and burn it
night and day at your shrine,
O my beloved.
For your love I shall sacrifice all the wealth of my youth;
Your name shall be the crown of my head.
I am longing for you, O my love: for the season of my sowing
has come: . . .

So great a fire burned in Mirabai's heart that she would cry out in prayers to the Divine Beloved like a person who has fallen madly in love and no longer wants anything in life but union with him. When he is gone, when he is absent, nothing else matters, nothing on earth will satisfy the yearning for even one more night with "The Dark One," the Holy Source of her tender feelings and passionate flame. When she is feeling abandoned and desolate, she begs him in poem after poem to come back to her: "Come to my bedroom," she writes, "I've scattered fresh buds on the couch; perfumed my body; . . . I am yours, sleep only with you."

Like Mirabai waiting for God, all lovers must wait at times for a beloved who distances, disappears, betrays, or in a thousand small ways forgets the sacredness of commitment, the obligations of sacred relationship. But in the spiritual life, each hurtful incident becomes a test: a test of compassion, patience, forgiveness, and trust. The spirituality of erotic love requires *compassion* for flaws and miscommunications; *patience* when the other is insensitive; *forgiveness* for neglect, possessiveness, selfishness, or jealousy; and *trust* in the beloved and in life.

For those who have truly fallen in love, who have learned to relate to each other totally—in body and spirit and mind and soul—who have willingly given their all to the great undertaking of committed love, every challenge is like the refiner's fire that heats, melts, burns, and sears to create a precious jewel. Each obstacle is a reminder that we are changeable, that we can grow and be transformed, that broken things can mend, that shattered relationships can be repaired. Each conflict tests our ability to heal—and our belief in healing. Each healing can take us to deeper and deeper levels of love, undreamed-of insights, unheard-of understanding.

For it is in the winter of a love affair that the work of the spiritual life begins. When summer warmth diminishes and nights grow cold, when the sun and moon and stars seem to lose their sheen, and trees have lost their green radiance, the spirit has no recourse but to plunge all the way to the ground of love, to the sacred depths where Divine light shimmers in darkness and the heart can open to its fullest breadth. In the winter of love, a partner can become the life's companion with whom we grow whole and old and beautiful, the one with whom even daily routine takes on meaning and shines in spiritual light. And it is then, when our roots have grown strong and secure in shared memories and experience, that we can know the beauty of lasting love—the contented, reliable, ever-increasing love that keeps us young in spirit and alive in the promise of spring.

Unending Love

I seem to have loved you in numberless forms, numberless times,
In life after life, in age after age forever.
My spell-bound heart has made and re-made the necklace of songs
That you take as a gift, wear round your neck in your many forms
In life after life, in age after age forever.

Whenever I hear old chronicles of love, its age-old pain,
its ancient tale of being apart or together,
As I stare on and on into the past, in the end you emerge
Clad in the light of a pole-star piercing the darkness of time:
You become an image of what is remembered forever.

You and I have floated here on the stream that brings from the
    fount
At the heart of time love for one another.
We have played alongside millions of lovers, shared in the same
Shy sweetness of meeting, the same distressful tears of farewell—
Old love, but in shapes that renew and renew forever.

Today it is heaped at your feet, it has found its end in you,
The love of all man's days both past and forever:
Universal joy, universal sorrow, universal life,
The memories of all loves merging with this one love of ours—
And the songs of every poet past and forever.

                                    Rabindranath Tagore; India, 1861-1941

54

O, LOVE

O, love, O pure deep love, be here, be now
Be all; worlds dissolve into your stainless endless radiance,
Frail living leaves burn with you brighter than cold stars:
Make me your servant, your breath, your core.

Jalal al-Din Rumi, Persia, 1207-1273

PARIS AND HELEN

He called her: golden dawn
She called him: the wind whistles

He called her: heart of the sky
She called him: message bringer

He called her: mother of pearl,
    barley woman, rice provider,
    millet basket, corn maid,
    flax princess, all-maker, weef

She called him: fawn, roebuck,
    stag, courage, thunderman
    all-in-green, mountain strider,
    keeper of forest, my-love-rides

He called her: the tree is
She called him: bird dancing

He called her: who stands,
    has stood, will always stand
She called him: arriver

He called her: the heart and the womb
    are similar
She called him: arrow in my heart.
Judy Grahn; United States, twentieth century

ONLY YOU

No being in all the wide realms of heaven
or across this vast earth
can understand my desperate longing.

Only You.
Only You.

Ramprasad Sen, Bengal, 1718-1775

Bring News of My Beloved

O whispering breeze, bring news of my beloved Shams.
It would be worth more than all the amber and musk from China
    to Constantinople,
Tell me, tell me if you heard a word from his sweet lips or a beat
    from his pounding heart.
O just one word from Shams and I would gladly give my life.
His life is before me and behind me, and through his love, my
    heart has become pure, my breast has imbibed every virtue,
One smell of his perfume and I walk light-headed on this path,
O cupbearer, enough of your wine, I am drunk on the wine from
    his cup.
My nose is so full of his fragrance that I have no need for incense,
    musk, or the fine amber of Mongolia.
Shams-ud-Din is alive forever in my heart,
Shams-ud-Din is the generosity of every soul,
Shams-ud-Din is poverty, Shams-ud-Din is the purest of all wealth,
I am not the only one singing Shams-ud-Din, Shams-ud-Din;
The nightingales sing it from the garden and the partridge from the
    mountainside.
The beauty of a starry night is Shams-ud-Din.
The garden of Paradise is Shams-ud-Din;
Love, compassion, and gratitude, all, all, are Shams-ud-Din
Shams-ud-Din is the brightness of day,
Shams-ud-Din is the turning sky,
Shams-ud-Din is time everlasting,
Shams-ud-Din is the endless treasure,
Shams-ud-Din is the King of cups,
Shams-ud-Din is the Ocean of nectar,

Shams-ud-Din is the breath of Jesus,
Shams-ud-Din is the face of Joseph,
O God, show me that inner place where we can sit together,
Shams in the middle, my soul by his side,
Shams-ud-Din is sweeter than life,
Shams-ud-Din is a hearth full of sugar,
Shams-ud-Din is the towering cypress,
Shams-ud-Din is the flowering spring,
Shams-ud-Din is the world of clear water . . .
Shams-ud-Din is the barrel of wine,
Shams-ud-Din is the bliss of my soul,
O Shams, you are the hope of every heart,
The one that every lover longs to hear.
O Shams, come back, come back, don't leave my soul in ruins.

Jalal al-Din Rumi; Persia, 1207–1273

A Dream

In a dream
At night
I saw the face
Of my Beloved!

Ah, what a sight!
Kabir, India, 1450-1518

Savitri's First Meeting with Satyavan

So he appeared against the forest verge
Inset twixt green relief and golden ray.
As if a weapon of the living light,
Erect and lofty like a spear of God,
His figure led the splendour of the morn. . . .
Sri Aurobindo, India, 1872-1950

The Dark Night of the Soul

Upon a darkened night,
With all my cares to loving ardours flushed,
(O windfall of delight!)
With nobody in sight
I went abroad when all my house was hushed.

In safety, in disguise,
In darkness up the secret stair I crept,
(O happy enterprise!)
Concealed from other eyes,
When all my house at length in silence slept.

Upon a lucky night
In secrecy, inscrutable to sight,
I went without discerning
And with no other light
Except for that which in my heart was burning.

It lit and led me through
More certain than the light of noonday clear
To where One waited near
Whose presence well I knew,
There where no other presence might appear.

O night that was my guide!
O night more lovely than the rising sun,
O night that joined the lover
To the beloved one

Transfiguring them each into the other.
Within my flowering breast
Which only for himself entire I save
He sank into his rest
And all my gifts I gave
Lulled by the airs with which the cedars wave.

Over the ramparts fanned
While the fresh wind was fluttering his tresses,
With his serenest hand
My neck he wounded, and
Suspended every sense with its caresses.

Lost to myself I stayed
My face upon my lover having laid
From all endeavour ceasing:
And all my cares releasing
Threw them among the lilies there to fade.

John of the Cross; Spain, c. 1342-c. 1413

She Said She Would Come

She said she would come
At once, and so I waited
Till the moon rose
In the October dawn.

The monk Sosei; Japan, ninth century

This Separation

I am thirsting for your love, O my beloved,
I shall make this body a lamp, and my tender heart shall be its
    wick;
I shall fill it with the scented oil of my young love
    and burn it night and day at your shrine,
    O my beloved.
For your love I shall sacrifice all the wealth of my youth;
Your name shall be the crown of my head.
I am longing for you, O my love: for the season of my
    sowing has come:
    but you are not beside me.
Clouds gather on my brows and my eyes shed heavy showers.
I have given myself to you: I have become yours forever:
    who but you can be my love?
This separation troubles my breast; make me your own,
    O perfect love.

Mirabai; India, 1498-1550

LOVE PRAYER
(With a tip-of-the-hat to Coleman Barks)

Oh, God(dess)
Grant me love!

Please, make it simply
Difficult.
Make it crack and melt the hard places
Where I am so sure of myself.

Make it stiffen and enliven the weak places
Where I am uncertain, ignorant,
and secretly afraid.

And please make it horribly "inappropriate"
So I must really know you in myself,
Myself in you,
Forced
To give up everything that is not love
(Because it is so hard to do it willingly . . .)

I pray this
Knowing it will ruin me.

Let me be ruined by love,
So that I may come back to you
Without pride, or stupidity,
Or pretense, or opinions—or any sense of separation—

Stripped
Like a lover,
Hungry and ecstatically full
All at the same time!
Jeremy Taylor; United States, twentieth century

What Do You Want of Me?

Beloved, what do you want of me?
I contain all that was, and that is, and shall be,
I am filled with the all.
Take of me all you please—
if you want all of myself, I'll not say no.
Tell me, beloved, what you want of me. . . .

Marguerita Porete; France, ?-1310
Translated by Peter Dronke

My Lover

My Lover—
How shall I
Describe His face?
Who would believe
My words, anyway? . . .

Kabir; India, 1450-1518

O Living Flame of Love

O living flame of love
That tenderly wounds my soul
In its deepest center! Since
Now you are not oppressive,
Now Consummate! If it be your will:
Tear through the veil of this sweet encounter!

O sweet cautery,
O delightful wound!
O gentle hand! O delicate touch
That tastes of eternal life
And pays every debt!
In killing you changed death to life.

O lamps of fire!
In whose splendors
The deep caverns of feeling,
Once obscure and blind,
Now give forth, so rarely, so exquisitely,
Both warmth and light to their beloved.

How gently and lovingly
You wake in my heart,
Where in secret you dwell alone;
And in your sweet breathing,
Filled with good and glory,
How tenderly you swell my heart with love.

John of the Cross; Spain, c. 1342-c. 1413

CLOSE TO THE HOLY ONE

O You whose face illuminates
    my dark room,
this moth encircling your body
    is my heart

Source unknown; Persia,
c. thirteenth century

I FIND HER NOT

In desperate hope I go and search for her in all the corners of my
    room; I find her not.
My house is small and what once has gone from it can never be
    regained.
But infinite is your mansion, my lord, and seeking her I have come
    to your door.
I stand under the golden canopy of your evening sky and lift my
    eager eyes to your face.
I have come to the brink of eternity from which nothing can
    vanish—no hope, no happiness, no vision of a face seen through
    tears.
Oh, dip my emptied life into that ocean, plunge it into the deepest
    fullness. Let me for once feel that lost sweet touch in the allness
    of the universe.

Rabindranath Tagore; India, 1861–1941

My Beautiful Love as Yet Unknown

My beautiful love as yet unknown
   you are living and breathing
   somewhere far away or perhaps quite close to me,
but I still know nothing
   of the threads that form the fabric of your life
   or the pattern which makes your face distinctive.

My beautiful love as yet unknown,
   I would like you to think of me tonight
   as I am thinking of you—
not in a golden dream that is far from my real self,
but as I really am, a living person
   that cannot be invented without distorting the truth.

My beautiful love as yet unknown,
   I love you already although your face is hidden.
If I can make myself richer now
   I shall be able to enrich you
and I want to learn how to give
   rather than always to take.
When you enter my life and I recognise you,
   I do not want to take you like a thief.
I want to receive you like a treasure
and let you give yourself to me.

My beautiful love as yet unknown,
   will you forgive me in the future?

I hope you will forgive me
　　when you are curled up beside me
　　and when your eyes seek out the most distant clouds
　　in the open sky of my eyes.
I hope you will forgive me;
　　for knowing too well the gestures of love
　　because I have learned them from others before you.
　　I would like to forget them now for your sake!
How lovely it would be if we could seek and find together
　　the chords that would form the right accompaniment
　　to the songs of joy and suffering that we shall sing
　　　　　　　　　　　　　　　　　　　together!

My beautiful love as yet unknown,
　　I want to pray for you tonight
　　because you already exist,
　　because I already want to be faithful to you
　　and because you are already having difficulties
　　and possibly because of me.
I am preparing myself for you
　　and you are preparing yourself for me. . . .

My beautiful love as yet unknown,
　　we have to wait for one another now.
We know how painful it is for lovers
　　who do not know each other's faces
　　to go on waiting for each other!
But we also know that, although we are still apart,
　　our two lives are looking and calling for each other.

And I am also sure that, in the darkness of our longing,
   God's longing and his Light are present. . . .

Michel Quoist, France, twentieth century

YOU HAVE COME, MY BELOVED

You have come, my beloved,
The clouds are gone.
The wind is silent.
The sun appears,
and the trees are green.

Adapted from a poem by Tinh Thuy,
   South Vietnam, twentieth century

I Am Alone

The wild goose flies up, then settles,
    diving into the netting;
Birds scurry about like lizards,
    and I hurry [to calm them.]
I turn back bearing my love for you,
    for I am alone—
This heart of mine is counterpart to your own;
    I shall never be far from your charms.

From the Harris Papyrus; Ancient Egypt

A Druid Blessing of the Sacred Grove

May Rowan of the scarlet berries shield you,
and Ash protect you from the lightning flash.

May Oak be a door of strength for your departing,
and Willow weave a green bower for your returning.

May the Apple-branch of longing bear you to the Blessed Isles,
and the Birds of Rhiannon sing for you
where blossoms fall forever on the silver plain.

May Hawthorn flowers fill your heart
with the green fire of love in the wildwood.

May the Hazels of Wisdom drop their nuts in Connla's Well for
   you,
and may you glimpse the Salmon in its depths.

May slender Birch celebrate all your bright beginnings,
and Yew of Darkness fold you into the gathering dusk.

Mara Freeman; United States, twentieth century

TAKEN INTO ANOTHER'S LIFE

. . . And Satyavan looked out from his soul's doors
And felt the enchantment of her liquid voice
Fill his youth's purple ambiance and endured
The haunting miracle of a perfect face.
Mastered by the honey of a strange flower-mouth,
Drawn to soul-spaces opening round a brow,
He turned to the vision like a sea to the moon
And suffered a dream of beauty and of change,
Discovered the aureole round a mortal's head,
Adored a new divinity in things.
His self-bound nature foundered as in fire;
His life was taken into another's life.

Sri Aurobindo; India, 1872-1950

THE FLAMES OF YOUR LOVE

. . . Do not blame me if I gamble
   my life on your path;
What could I do?
   it was all I owned.

                I would set fire to
                    the tree of life
                If I could snatch one burning branch
                  from the flames of your
                    love. . . .

Khusrawi; Persia, d. 1920

FOR NOW ANOTHER REALM DRAWS NEAR

For now another realm draws near with you
And now diviner voices fill my ear;
A strange new world swims to me in your gaze
Approaching like a star from unknown heavens;
A cry of spheres comes with you and a song
Of flaming gods.

Sri Aurobindo; India, 1872-1950

THE ONE WHOM YOU SEEK IS WITH YOU

Lovers: The One Whom you seek
   is with you
Search within and without,
   He is with you.

At each breath He sets
   a lover's exam
and if you pass the test
   He is with you.

The soul's inmost secret is lit
   with His grace
I have seen the middle of the secret:
   He is with you.

The people of the heart have sacrificed
   their heads and purses
Appreciate this free offer:
   He is with you.
                     Shah Ni'mattullah; Syria, 1331–?

One Look from You

One look from you, and I look
At you in all things
Looking back at me; those eyes
In which all things live and burn.
Jalal al-Din Rumi, Persia, 1207-1273

Sonnet XI

Not in a silver casket cool with pearls
Or rich with red corundum or with blue,
Locked, and the key withheld, as other girls
Have given their loves, I give my love to you;
Not in a lovers'-knot, not in a ring
Worked in such fashion, and the legend plain—
Semper Fidelis, where a secret spring
kennels a drop of mischief for the brain:
Love in the open hand, no thing but that,
Ungemmed, unhidden, wishing not to hurt,
As one should bring you cowslips in a hat
Swung from the hand, or apples in her skirt,
I bring you, calling out as children do:
"Look what I have!—And these are all for you."
Edna St. Vincent Millay, United States, 1892-1950

To Work with Love

. . . to weave the cloth with threads drawn from your heart,
even as if your beloved were to wear that cloth;
It is to build a house with affection,
even as if your beloved were to dwell in that house.
It is to sow seeds with tenderness and reap the harvest with
joy, even as if your beloved were to eat the fruit.

Khalil Gibran; Lebanon, 1883–1931

The Confirmation

Yes, yours my love, is the right human face
I in my mind had waited for this long,
Seeing the false and searching for the true,
Then found you as a traveler finds a place
Of welcome suddenly amidst the wrong
Valleys and rocks and twisting roads. But you,
What shall I call you? A fountain in a waste,
A well of water in a country dry,
Or anything that's honest and good, an eye
That makes the whole world bright. Your open heart,
Simple with giving, gives the primal deed,
The first good world, the blossom, the blowing seed,
The hearth, the steadfast land, the wandering sea,
Not beautiful or rare in every part,
But like yourself, as they were meant to be.

Edwin Muir; Scotland, 1887–1959

ON THE DAY I FIRST LOVED YOU

On the day I first loved you I swore by my soul
    and renounced my heart and religion.
Last night in sighing for those wet-ruby lips
    I embroidered my robe with tears of pearl.
My heart was lost in the land of desire;
    two hundred times I prostrated, eyes in the dust.
And yet, on that first day I was not so bewildered as now;
    I have fallen in this trap thinking of your dark hair.
In love of you, the only face of beauty in this world,
    I have coupled with sorrow, wounded by separation.
O preacher, blame me not for worshipping Love;
    many of your sort have advised me, but I heard them not.

Munis 'Ali Shah; Iran, 1778-1853

IN LOVE WITH HIM

In love with him, my soul
Lives the subtlest of passions,
Lives like a gypsy
Each day a different house.
Each night under the stars.

Jalal al-Din Rumi; Persia, 1207-1273

But Perhaps God Needs the Longing

But perhaps God needs the longing, wherever else should it dwell,

Which with kisses and tears and sighs fills mysterious spaces of
air—

And perhaps is invisible soil from which roots of stars grow and
swell—

And the radiant voice across fields of parting which calls to reunion
there?

O my beloved, perhaps in the sky of longing worlds have been born
of our love—

Just as our breathing, in and out, builds a cradle for life and death?

We are grains of sand, dark with farewell, lost in birth's secret
treasure trove,

Around us already perhaps future moons, suns, and stars blaze in a
fiery wreath.

Nelly Sachs: Germany, 1891–1970
Translated by Ruth and Matthew Mead

LOVERS AND MEN OF INTELLECT

Lovers and men of intellect cannot mix:
How can you mix the broken with the unbroken?
Cautious men of intellect shrink back from a dead ant:
Lovers, completely carefree, trample down dragons.

The intellect says: "The six directions are limits: there is no way
    out."
Love says: "There is a way: I have traveled it thousands of times."
The intellect saw a market and started to haggle:
Love saw thousands of markets beyond that market.
Lovers who drink the dregs of the wine reel from bliss to bliss:
The dark-hearted men of reason
Burn inwardly with denial.
The intellect says: "Do not go forward, annihilation contains only
    thorns."
Love laughs back: "The thorns are in you."
Enough words! Silence!
Pull the thorn of existence out of the heart! Fast!
For when you do you will see thousands of rose gardens in yourself.

Jalal al-Din Rumi; Persia, 1207-1273

SURRENDER

I look everywhere for you, my beloved,
and you assure me: you are always here.

I search for your scent in the crowd,
and you whisper in my ear: I am here, I am here.

I am a pilgrim searching for your face,
And you reveal: the cosmos is your temple.

I scour libraries and sit at scholars' feet in search of wisdom,
and you teach me: the truth lies within.

I am hungry for a sex that will satiate my passion,
and you echo: embrace yourself and be fulfilled.

I seek the immutable law of black and white,
and softly you proclaim: obey those commandments that rise in
    your heart.

Hungry, I gorge my soul with experience,
and you advise: emptiness is the means and the attainment.

I invested in profit and loss,
and you disclosed: Love is riches, abundant and free.

I was betrayed by friends and lovers, left broken and cynical,
and you reminded: trust, trust, trust.

I worked hard, strained in devotion, and maintained my vigil,
and you laughed: let grace happen.

I hid from my mortality, and purchased insurance,
while you underwrote: die in each moment and be reborn.

I made plans and secured options,
you hinted: tomorrow never comes.

Finally my will ran into the wall,
without recourse, without backup, broken, frustrated, spent,
I was STOPPED in my tracks,
and you came to me: open your eyes and see.

Michael Ziegler, United States, twentieth century

Two Hermits in One House

When we were young—bashful, yet beautiful—
we walked hand in hand across the hills of
Ulster, whispering words of love to one another.

I had known you since we were both aged
seven, and I had watched you grow into a
maiden of rare beauty; to look upon you was
like gazing onto heaven itself.

When we married we lived a simple, blameless
life, working hard during the day, and enjoying
one another at night; I shall always remember
the happiness of those early years.

You bore five children, and I toiled in the
fields to feed them: I shall always thank God
that he provided enough for our needs.

Now our children are adults, our bodies are
old and wrinkled, and the taste of pleasure
fades, the joys of this world grow less, so the
joys of prayer grow greater.

Let us be companions on the pilgrimage of
prayer, let us be brother and sister before the altar of God.

As the darkness of age covers our faces, let
the light of heaven penetrate our souls.

We shall be two hermits in one house, two
souls devoted to one God.

Celtic oral tradition; England, Ireland, Scotland,
Wales, first millennium

THE MYSTICAL SIDE TO COMPASSION

If the soul is where God works compassion, then we have soul only
to the extent that we have become instruments for the divine
compassion. No compassion, no soul. Yet compassion is not
about pity or dropping crumbs from a table. Rather, it is about
entering fully into our shared interdependence, whether that
sharing is by way of rejoicing or whether it is about suffering and
anguish. To follow one another into joy and to celebrate—to
stand together with one another in grief and to struggle against
injustice—these are the two directions of compassion. What
Mechthild of Magdeburg called the "white wine" of joy, the "red
wine" of sorrow. Compassion emerges from such a hot passion
that it allows boundaries of ego and separation to melt long
enough to enter into one another's deep spaces. There all
becomes one.

Matthew Fox; United States, twentieth century

Chapter 3

Spiritual Friendship

*I*n the great era of sacred friendship, the mid-twelfth century, a poet described the one person with whom he could exchange all the secrets of his heart as his "faithful, close, complete, constant friend." In the same era, the beloved Abbot Aelred of Rievaulx turned his monastery into a true community of friendships where people could take time to shape relationships as carefully and lovingly as the artists creating the great cathedrals of Chartres and Cologne. Like the brilliant stained glass windows and sculpted portals at those holy sites, a friendship was a work of art that radiated beauty, grace, and inspiration.

Friends brought out the best and wisest in one another and met one another's most essential needs by mirroring the intrinsic beauty in the other's soul; by sharing interests in deep, refined conversations, empowering one another through mutual support and commitment, accepting each other's flaws in the context of the spirit and their innate integrity. In the twelfth century, the ideal of spiritual friendship provided motivation to never "use" another, but instead to connect in the spirit, to enjoy the finer things of life together, willing to spend and be spent for the sake of one's friend.

A prayer written by the medieval mystic, Richard Rolle, expresses the sweetness shared by intimate friends:

Your friendship is my glory.
When I began to love you,
your hand held up my whole heart,

And I found myself wanting nothing and no one
more than you.
In you and through you I felt I could suffer
any pain, any indignity, without anguish.
Your warmth melted my stubborn pride,
and your sweetness carried away my sadness.
I put my trust in you,
knowing that I could be happy with you forever.

At an earlier time in his life, Rolle had prayed with the poignant
longing and loneliness of alienated twentieth-century people: "If only
you would send me a companion for my journey . . . I would be so
happy. I would sing your praises and would be so grateful for honest
and positive conversation. . . . The very eating of our meals would
be enjoyed in love."

In the thirteenth century, Thomas Aquinas was teaching that
friendship is the end and goal of all ethics. For Aquinas, as for more
and more people in the West today who are experiencing the redis-
covery of spirit and are rapidly recovering the lost art of friendship,
there is no higher ethical act than to treat another as a friend—and to
treat that friend as a valued, esteemed, respected, trusted, and beloved
person whose vulnerabilities we shelter, whose sensitivities we protect.

As more and more people imitate the medieval ideal of spiritual
friendship, as the ideal of spiritual friendship becomes more and more
the model for human relationships, it is possible to imagine a new
world full of grace where people are friends who meet, communicate,
create, enjoy, and work in the spirit of mutual love.

What Is It You Seek?

What is it you seek
O my friend?
You would find only
What you seek!
If you are
Truly thirsty,
Remember:
Some drops of dew
Would not satisfy
Your thirst:
You must dive into
The river!
Kabir, India, 1450-1518

THE SIGHT OF YOUR FACE IS A BLESSING

Don't hide. The sight of your face is a blessing.
Wherever you place your foot, there rests a blessing
Even your shadow
Passing over me like a swift bird
Is a blessing
The great spring has come
Your sweet air, blowing through the city,
The country, the gardens
And the deserts are a blessing
He has come with love to our door
His knock is a blessing.

Jalal al-Din Rumi; Persia, 1207-1273

WE HAVE NOT STOPPED PRAYING FOR YOU

Since the day we first heard about you, we have not stopped
praying for you and asking God to fill you with knowledge of his
will through all spiritual wisdom and understanding. And we pray
this in order that you may have a life worthy of the Lord and
may please God in every way: bearing fruit in every good work,
growing in the knowledge of God, being strengthened with all
power according to God's glorious power, so that you may have
great endurance and patience, and joyfully giving thanks to the
Father, who has qualified you to share in the inheritance of the
saints in the kingdom of light.

Colossians 1:9-12

Plum Flowers

Plum flowers
comfort
an old man's heart!
My friend of past times
isn't here anymore.

The Zen monk, Ryokan; Japan, 1758-1831
Translated by Burton Watson

Every Time I Remember You

I thank my God every time I remember you. In all my prayers for
all of you, I always pray with joy because of your partnership in
the good news from the first until now, being confident of this,
that he who began a good work in you will carry it on to
completion until the day of Christ Jesus.

Philippians 1:9-11

FOR THE HEALING OF A FRIEND

O most merciful God and mighty Father,
we most humbly beseech you,
if it be your good pleasure,
to continue to us that singular benefit
which you have given us
in the friendship of your servant,
our dear brother,
who now lies on the bed of sickness.
Let him abide with us yet awhile
for the furtherance of our faith;
yet awhile spare him,
that he may live to your honour and our comfort.
You have made him a great help
and furtherance of the best things among us.
O, Lord, we beseech you
restore us our dear brother,
by restoring him to health.

Nicholas Ferrar, England, 1592-1637
For the healing of the priest and poet George Herbert, during a serious illness

Because You Are Love

You love with an everlasting love because you are love. And so you
are patiently effective always and everywhere, even when we
cannot feel your presence. Teach us to love without wanting to
control; to love without limit; to love you, our friends, and also
our enemies. Teach us to be patient in love when love is not
returned; teach us to be patient when even you are apparently far
away. Teach us loving, waiting, patience when there is no answer
to our questionings and our doubt.

Michael Hollings and Etta Gullick; England, twentieth century

A Prayer for a Friend's Recovery

O great Deng, let her live,
Let her recover and escape from death,
O great Deng, let her live!

The Dinka people of the Sudan; traditional

The Joy of Giving

Teach us, O God, that we who are so used to receiving the bounty
of others are missing the most of life, if we do not learn the joy
of giving. We make our friends happier by giving, and happy
friends are themselves the best of God's gifts. We make the world
better by the gift of our service and our selves, and it is a better
world that we ourselves need. So in some mystic way does God
bring this realization through sacrifice and this is the greatest
lesson youth may learn. Amen.

Acts 20:31-36

Living with Wisdom

For God loves nothing
so much as the person
who lives with wisdom.
She is more beautiful
than the sun, and excels
every constellation
of the stars.
The Wisdom of Solomon 7:28-29

My child, would God that I, your faithful father, could die for you, my dear and good child. Though I do not die in the body, my heart is dying for the child I love in my heart. It is true that I am not with you in the body, but my heart is at your deathbed and weeps bitterly and makes constant lament. Give me your feeble hand. And, if God bids you, die gladly and be firm in faith. Rejoice that your beautiful soul, which is a pure and reasonable spirit shaped to the pattern of God, is to be released and will then joyfully savour its blessedness without any hindrance, for God Himself says: "There shall no man see me and live."

My child, turn your heart, and hands, and eyes toward your heavenly home and greet it with an avid heart, and commend your will to the will of God. Let not your soul be troubled. Whatever God may have in store for you, be it life or death, accept it as what is best, since it comes from God. For, although you may not know it at the moment, it is best. Do not be afraid: the holy angels are around you and with you. God, who is gentle and compassionate, will help you out of your anguish as a father; if you only trust in His goodness.

Heinrich Suso; Germany, 1300-1366

Art Thou Abroad?

Art thou abroad on this stormy night on
    the journey of love, my friend? The sky
    groans like one in despair.
I have no sleep tonight. Ever and again
    I open my door and look out on the
    darkness, my friend!
I can see nothing before me. I wonder
    where lies thy path!
By what dim shore of the ink-black
    river, by what far edge of the frowning
    forest, through what mazy depth of gloom
    art thou threading thy course to come to
    me, my friend?

Rabindranath Tagore; India, 1861–1941

A Man Without Friends

Let me take you inside the soul of a rich man without love, and a
    wealthy man without friends.
The darkest night, with neither moon nor stars, is like the brightest
    day compared with the darkness of this soul.
The coldest winter, with thick snow and hard ice, is like the
    warmest summer compared with the coldness of this soul.
The bleakest mountain, bare and swept by gales, is like the lushest
    meadow compared with the bleakness of this soul.

Celtic oral tradition; England, Ireland, Scotland, Wales, first millennium

My God,

Be my Ally so that You may help me and others through me.
Enrich me with Your kindness, so that, content with You,
I can do without asking for anything. You are the one who makes
the lights shine in the hearts of Your saints so that they know
You and affirm Your Oneness. You are the one who makes alterities
disappear from the hearts of Your lovers so that they love none
but You and take refuge in none but You. You are the one who
befriends them when the world makes them forlorn. You are the
one who guides them till the landmarks become clear for them.
Those who have lost You—what love have they found?
Those who have found You—what have they lost?
Whoever takes someone other than You as a substitute
is disappointed, and whoever wants to stray away from You
is lost.

Ibn 'Ata' Illah, Egypt, thirteenth century

Where Did You Come From?

Where did you come from,
following dream paths
through the night to reach me
these deep mountains
still heaped high with snow?

The Zen monk, Ryokan; Japan, 1758-1831
Translated by Burton Watson

A Prayer for Brother Leo

God bless you and keep you.
May God smile on you, and be merciful to you;
May God turn his regard toward you
   and give you peace.
May God bless you, Brother Leo.

Francis of Assisi; Italy, 1182-1226

In Time of Betrayal

I have told you all about my life, O God,
and my tears have moved your heart.
All who hate me whisper together about me
discussing what to do.
They have repaid my kindness with evil
and my friendship with hatred.
In return for my friendship they slandered me;
all I could do was pray.
My holy Father, King of heaven and earth.
do not desert me for I am in trouble
and I have no one to help me.
When I call on you,
my enemies fall back;
now I know that God is with me.
My friends and companions
keep their distance
because of my affliction.
Holy God, do not desert me,
my God, hasten to help me.
Come quickly to my help,
Lord God.

Roman Catholic; traditional

Equal to Friends and Enemies

One who is equal to friends and enemies, who is balanced in honor and dishonor, heat and cold, happiness and distress, fame and infamy, who is always free from contamination, always silent and satisfied with anything, who doesn't care for any residence, who is fixed in knowledge and engaged in devotional service, is very dear to Me.

Bhagavad-gita 12, 18-19; India, c. 200 B.C.

I Saw in Louisiana a Live-Oak Growing

I saw in Louisiana a live-oak growing,
All alone stood it, and the moss hung down from the branches;
Without any companion it grew there, uttering joyous leaves of dark
    green,
And its look, rude, unbending, lusty, made me think of myself;
But I wonder'd how it could utter joyous leaves, standing alone
    there, without its friend, its lover near—for I knew I could not;
And I broke off a twig with a certain number of leaves upon it,
    and twined around it a little moss,
And brought it away—and I have placed it in sight in my room;
It is not needed to remind me as of my own dear friends,
(For I believe lately I think of little else than of them:) . . .

Walt Whitman; United States, 1819-1892

LET US GO TO THE FRIEND

It is the day of great, great joy,
Let us all now, become friends.
Let us join our hands. Let us go to the Friend.
We are all one, we are not two of one color and hue.

Jalal al-Din Rumi, Persia, 1207-1273

THE PLEASURE OF FRIENDSHIP

Do not abandon old
friends, for new ones
cannot equal them.
A new friend is like
new wine; when it has
aged, you will drink it
with pleasure.

Sirach 9:10

I Long to See You

I am grateful to God—
Whom I worship
with a clear conscience,
as my ancestors did—
when I remember you in my prayers
constantly
day and night.
Recalling your tears
I long to see you
so that I may be filled with joy.

2 Timothy 1:34

Deep Peace of the Shining Star to You

Deep peace of the shining star to you,
Deep peace of the running wave to you,
Deep peace of the quiet earth to you,
Deep joy of the leaping fire to you,
Deep peace of the Son of Peace to you.

Celtic oral tradition; England, Ireland, Scotland,
Wales, first millennium

Chapter 4

Family
Love

Collective ancestral wisdom has always passed on—and still passes on, in all indigenous cultures throughout the world—a sacred vision of family love. Parents and brothers, sisters, cousins of all degrees, grandmothers, grandfathers, all living relatives help one another, nurture, inspire, encourage, hear and speak caring words. From birth until death, each day is in a way a ritual of relatedness, a celebration of connectedness that commemorates life-together, mourns the sorrow of life alone. A sacred poem by the Zen monk, Ryokan, shows how tenderly family members can love one another. In this poem, a young man recalls the priceless value of a simple gift from his devoted little brother:

> . . . a piece of tanned leather
> white and clean
> as tapa cloth,
> this leather
> I look on
> as the treasure of my house—
> I wrap it round me
> when I venture abroad,
> make it my coverlet
> when I go to bed,
> never a moment
> parted from my side. . . .
> right on top of it . . .

[I] find I sleep soundly
all night long,
warm and basky
in dead-of-winter months
snug as though
I were welcoming spring days!

Through a supremely humble gift, a young man lights a fire of love that blesses his brother's life with warmth and security.

In the contemporary West, similarly deep family love is notable in a story set in Vietnam in the 1960s:

Sleepless and traumatized by the horror of combat, a young American captain sought help from his unit's chaplain. Describing his anguish and loss and the pain of unrelenting fear, the young captain paused to remark that from time to time he felt a surprising, pervasive sense of peace that made no sense in light of his situation. "Could it be," the chaplain asked him, "that someone at home is praying for you?"

"Yes! Of course!" came the immediate answer. "My mother."

It is very powerful for family members to pray for one another.

Like the mystical body comprising all humankind, the family is an image of the whole, a miniature imitation of the great cosmos that holds all beings together in one holy love. Invisibly interconnected, bonded, related, like the threads in a sacred robe, we are born into family communities to protect, support, encourage, inspire, warm one another in a circle of ever-widening love.

Memories of My Mother

Memories of my mother
morning and evening
I look
far off at those
island shores of Sado

The Zen monk, Ryokan;
Japan, 1758-1831
Translated by Burton Watson

A Gift of Remembrance

Gift of Spirit that I am.

I am called this morning
to this ancient place
of solitude
and silence

Called by ancient ancestral voices
from a deeply
troubling sleep

Called once again
to this place of whispered
remembrances
where the sacred voices
of long-forgotten
ancestors
rustle silently through
these ancient and
endangered groves

Summoned by these
ancient grandmothers
to this most holy place
to bear witness
to the first faint rays
of another dawn

Please grant us
in Your grace
the gift of wisdom
that we may remember
even at this late hour
to love
to honor
to protect
and defend
the most precious
of Your many gifts,
our children.

Belvie Rooks, United States,
twentieth century

A Child's Blessing for His Parents

Heavenly God! to you I owe the happiness of still possessing my
dear parents. You have preserved them to me in your love: they
are to me on earth what you are in heaven to all Your children,
and their tenderness is a ray of Your divine love. Your law, the
source of every noble sentiment, ordains that we should love
them, so that they should never fail to be the most sacred objects
of our respect and veneration here below. How many sacrifices do
they make for our happiness! What care, what anxiety do we cost
them! But their kindness and solicitude are unlimited. They are
as angels placed near us by you, O God! to guide and confirm us
in doing good by their counsels and example. O my God!
lengthen their days; preserve them yet a long time to us their
children; grant us the happiness of surrounding them with marks
of our love and veneration for many years yet to come, and to
comfort and cheer them in their old age. Remove sorrow and
affliction far from them, and grant them prosperity and robust
health of body; grant them the blessing bestowed on the
Patriarchs, so that they may live to the most advanced age in
gladness and peace.

May I through my deeds bring joy to their hearts and honor to
their name; and let your grace enable me to realize this desire in
obedience to your holy law, the source of every righteous
sentiment. Amen.

Jewish; traditional

FATHER'S NETS ARE FILLED

Lord,
I sing your praise,
The whole day through until the night.
Father's nets are filled,
I have helped him.
We have drawn them in,
Stamping the rhythm with our feet,
the muscles tense.
We have sung your praise.
On the beach, there were our mothers,
Who brought the blessing out of the nets,
Out of the nets into their basins.
They rushed to the market,
Returned and brought again.
Lord, what a blessing is the sea
With fish in plenty.
Lord, that is the story of your grace.
Nets tear, and we succumb
Because we cannot hold them.
Lord, with your praise we drop off to sleep.
Carry us through the night,
Make us fresh for the morning.
Hallelujah for the day!
And blessing for the night!
Amen.

Ghana, traditional

SONG OF FAREWELL TO A DYING FATHER

Where are you going, my father?
I am going to the great forest. I am going walking.
Why do you go? Who goes with you?
I go to harvest the sweet cocoa leaf, I go alone.
Come back soon, come back soon.
I will wait for you crying,
I will wait for you grieving.

In the woods where you must go
A black flag is waving.
In the open place that you must cross
The parting grass spreads cloaks of flowers.
What heart is this bitter heart
That leaves the dove?

Little bell of Paucartambo,
Ring farewell for me.
I am going to the great forest.
I will never return.

Quechua oral tradition; Peru
Translated by John Bierhorst

Dying at 31

Padre, my mother
Will be alone,
Please be her comforter
When I am gone.

Rosa of Lima; Peru,
1586-1617

The People Shall Stand as One

Behold the sacred hoop of your people,
the grandfathers and the great-grandfathers,
the young generations and the old.
From them, you shall have wisdom.
You shall walk again toward a good land,
And the people shall stand as one,
and all living creatures of the earth's generations
shall walk together as relatives.

Adapted from Black Elk, Oglala Sioux tradition;
Native America

Off-center and still shaken from the throw
onto the slowly spinning Potter's wheel,
the clay had scarcely time to wonder, so
quickly did the hands begin to feel
the shape and heal the cracks and now to shift
the hopeless lumpy mass back from the side
and, yes, into the center, and to lift
it toward a shape it had no need to hide.
To see the ragged edges smoothed at last,
to see a form emerge, new shape begun,
was finally to see the painful past
transformed into a new life for my son.
I cannot guide the hand, or see the face
of love the Potter has, but know her grace.

Margaret G. Payne; United States, twentieth century

I Am Always Right Beside You

All my children think I am far away, but I am always right beside
you. I never leave you. Never! Not even for a moment. If you
open your hearts, you will be able to recognize me. And you will
know how much I love you.

Source unknown

FAMILY SABBATH CELEBRATION

Come, let us welcome the Sabbath.
May its radiance illumine our hearts
as we kindle these tapers.

May the Lord bless us with Sabbath joy.
May the Lord bless us with Sabbath holiness.
May the Lord bless us with Sabbath peace.

Jewish Sabbath blessing; traditional

MOTHER, WHERE ARE YOU?

What of you, Mother, where are you?
You can't have forgotten me, surely?
When you sit outside on our roof beneath the new moon,
Do you still tell fairy-stories?
Or do you, alone in bed, lie awake at night,
In tears and sickness of heart?
Take flowers to the temple at dawn to offer your prayers
For your exiled daughter's well-being?
Here also the moon rises over the roof,
Its light is at my door and begs for entry.
I feel that it wandered widely before it found me,
It sought me because it loved me.

Rabindranath Tagore; India, 1861–1941

Evocation for the Soul of a Dead Man

Where are you?
Where have you gone?
Your family has come from far-away lands,
They, who were so close to you for all of your life, sit weeping in
   the hut.
Eyes filled with tears, they stare at the walls,
And recall the sweet life they had with you
And weep and wail, torn by so much pain.
The little children begotten of your body,
Cry out for you and sob:
"Father, where are you? Come back to us!"
Hear their cries and come back soon!

                       A-xurui!

All your brothers,
Your aged parents, the old ones of the village,
All your friends and companions
Are gathered here. Midst tears and prayers they are calling you.
You could return to them.
If you hear their entreaties and their calls,
Speedily return to your parents!

                       A-xurui! . . .

Your little horse is saddled
and awaits you.
Come, return to your little horse . . .
Come, the house
is all in order,
Shining splendidly.
Return

and claim it.
For many years
May you enjoy it . . .

     A-xurui!

Look!
The table is laid with your favorite delicacies:
With sweet-sour tarak,
With the nourishing amxan,
With the cooked salamat,
With golden yellow butter in great bowls
And whipped cream on the tarak.
Look! The cooked meat, the fat meat,
Ready on a plate.
And there is tea with sugar,
And there are sweetmeats.
Return and eat.
Enjoy these delicacies! . . .

     A-xurui!

Know this well:
The land of the dead
Is cold and dark and desolate.
While this shining world
Is warm and gay.
Therefore return.

    A-xurui—A-xurui—A-xurui

The Buryat people; Buryat autonomous region of Russia (Buryatiya); traditional

Our Daughter

I was present at her birth.
Her first cries voiced our joy.

Nestled in her mother's arms,
    She gazed intently at
two dumbstruck adoring strangers,
    gazing back at her.
        New to one another
we began a lifelong companionship
        of growing together.

    She continues to delight,
and often frustrate, as we must her.
        O precious daughter.

Ronald Y. Nakasone; United States, twentieth century

A Father's Worries

Lord my God
after my death what will become
of this your poor little family
which, of your goodness,
you have entrusted to me, a sinner?
Who will comfort them?
Who will correct them?
Who will pray to you for them?

Francis of Assisi; Italy, 1182-1226

Peace

Peace between neighbors,
Peace between kindred,
Peace between lovers,
    In the love of the God of Life.

Peace between person and person,
Peace between wife and husband,
Peace between women and children,
The peace of Christ above all peace.

Celtic oral tradition; Scotland, Wales,
England, Ireland, first millennium

When the day was approaching on which she was to depart this
life—a day that You knew though we did not—it came about, as
I believe by Your secret arrangement, that she and I stood alone
leaning in a window, which looked inwards to the garden within
the house where we were staying, at Ostia on the Tiber; for there
we were away from everybody, resting for the sea-voyage from the
weariness of our long journey by land. There we walked together,
she and I alone, in deep joy; and forgetting the things that were
behind and looking forward to those that were before, we were
discussing in the presence of Truth, which You are, what the
eternal life of the saints could be like, which eye has not seen
nor ear heard, nor has it entered into the heart of man. . . .

Rising as our love flamed upward towards that Holy Light, we
passed in review the various levels of bodily things, up to the
heavens themselves, whence sun and moon and stars shine upon
this earth. And higher still we soared, thinking in our minds and
speaking and marvelling at Your works: and so we came to our
own souls, and went beyond them to come at last to that region
of richness unending, from which You feed Israel forever with
the food of truth: and there life is that Wisdom by which all
things are made. . . . And while we were thus talking of Divine
Wisdom and longing for it, with all the effort of our heart, we
did for one instant attain to the vision of That-Which-Is. .

Augustine of Hippo; 354–430, North Africa

O Krsna, seeing my friends and relatives before me in a fighting spirit, I feel my body quivering and my mouth drying up. . . .

O Govinda, of what avail to us are kingdoms, happiness, or life itself when all those for whom we desire these are arrayed in a battlefield? O Medhersudhana, when teachers, fathers, sons and grandsons, uncles, fathers-in-law, and grandfathers, and brothers-in-law are willing to give up their lives, how could I see them die and wish to survive myself? O Maintainer of living beings, I would not fight in exchange for all worlds or planet earth.

Bhagavad-gita 30, 32-35; India, c. 200 B.C.

May peace be yours, dear friend of my youth! What gentle
memories and bitter regrets cluster around this tomb. Alas! death
claimed you too soon, and removed you too early from those
that loved you. What grief! to think that we, whom one roof
sheltered, one mother nourished, the same hearts cherished, and
the same hands blessed, are forever separated! We were so happy
together; your friendship was so sweet a support. Alas! your
departure has turned our joy into mourning. Nothing on earth is
lasting. I grieve in my selfishness at having lost you; but you are
happy near our Heavenly Creator, and this thought will inspire
me with courage and resignation, as likewise the glorious hope of
meeting you again in a better world, where eternal joy awaits the
righteous.

O my God! grant unto my brother's (sister's) soul the happiness of
the righteous; grant that, purified by death, he (she) may rejoice
in the beatitude of your divine presence. Amen.

Jewish; traditional

PRAYER FOR THE FAMILY

The sun has disappeared,
I have switched off the light,
and my wife and children are asleep.
The animals in the forest are full of fear,
and so are the people on their mats.
They prefer the day with your sun
to the night.
But I still know that your moon is
    there,
and your eyes and also your hands.
Thus I am not afraid.
This day again
you led us wonderfully.
Everybody went to his mat
satisfied and full.
Renew us during our sleep,
that in the morning
we may come afresh to our daily jobs.
Amen.

Anonymous, Ghana, twentieth century

As a Son

Unending one, you've shown yourself to me.

I love you as I would love a son
who long since went from me,
because his fate called him
to a high place
where he could see out
over all things.

Rainer Maria Rilke; Germany, 1875–1926

A Widow's Lament

It was in the night that I awoke, I, the woman, looking for the
founder of my nation, my lord, the precious man, the man I
love. And where do I hear him? Ah, the noble lord goes song-
weeping at Octepec. They've seized him in the scuffle, at the
gorge. In the Crimson now I seek you.
Ah, I'm grieving at my fireside, picking red feather-flowers. For
you. Have you reached the Shore, the Water's-Spreading-Out-
Place? Pass away adorned with these bereavement flowers that are
yours. I seek you.

Aztec; Mexico, traditional

LOVING ONE ANOTHER

O God of love, who hast given a new commandment that we
should love one another, even as you loved us, the unworthy and
the wandering, and gave your beloved . . . for our life and
salvation; we pray you Lord, give to us, your servants, in all time
of our life on the earth, a mind forgetful of past ill-will, a pure
conscience and sincere thoughts, and a heart to love our
brethren; for the sake of thy Son, our Lord.

Coptic Liturgy of Saint Cyril, Egypt,
fourth to fifth century,
formulated eighteenth to nineteenth century

FATHER AND MOTHER OF THE UNIVERSE

I am the father of this universe, the mother, the support, and the
grandsire. I am the object of knowledge, the purifier and the
syllable *om*.

Bhagavad-gita 9, 17; India, c. 200 B.C.

A SIMPLE FAMILY PRAYER

Good and gracious Creator, we thank you for the life and love you
have given us within the circle of our family. Grant us
understanding and spiritual energies in order to nurture this life
and love. We ask you to allow us a clearer focus on how best to
affirm and assist each other, especially when things are not going
just right. Grant us the grace to say what we must without
stepping on toes . . . showing our love in a growing way.
Frequently remind us that you are a loving and nurturing God.
Heal our moments of discouragement and increase our courage
through your presence in our lives. Send us your Spirit as our
guide. We thank you for the simple and awesome surprises of
happiness and hugs that continue to create our family life as it is
meant to be. Amen.

Thomas C. Abel; United States, twentieth century

Those I Have Tenderly Loved

Lord God,
We can hope for others nothing better
than the happiness we desire for ourselves.
Therefore, I pray You,
separate me not after death
from those I have tenderly loved on earth.
Grant, I pray you,
that where I am, they may be with me
and that I may enjoy their presence in heaven
after being so deprived of it on earth.
Lord God,
I ask You to receive Your beloved children
directly into Your life-giving heart.
After their brief life on earth,
give them eternal happiness.

Ambrose of Milan; Italy, c. 339-397

May Every Living Thing Be Full of Bliss

Now may every living thing, young or old, weak or strong, living
near or far, known or unknown, living or departed or yet
unborn, may every living thing be full of bliss.

The Buddha; India, c. 563-c. 483 B.C.

Chapter 5

Compassion

for

All

People

*O*nly a golden veil of shimmering light separates one being from another, one person from another, one people from another on the tiny celestial body known as "earth." Humanity, in all its various shapes and colors and sizes, is one in love, one in spirit, one in the work to be done in the world. Knowingly or unknowingly, we are all taking part together in a single great pilgrimage, sharing intimately— spiritually and physically—all that composes existence. "Every time a butterfly flaps its wings," a mystic has said, "every molecule in the cosmos moves." An atom of carbon in a hand is the same as one in a star. One holy, living Spirit indwells and infuses all beings equally. One throbbing pulse joins everything to everything.

This is the reason to "love one's neighbor as oneself," as all the world's scriptures teach. This is the reason to imagine at the side of everyone a holy messenger, like an angel of Fra Angelico, announcing: "Make way for Divinity."

When the distinguished Indian poet, Rabindranath Tagore, discovered the oneness of humankind, he wrote in ecstasy the following words:

> I found the world wrapt in an inexpressible glory with its waves of joy and beauty bursting and breaking on all sides. The thick cloud of sorrow that lay on my heart in many folds was pierced through and through by the light of the world, which was everywhere radiant. . . .
>
> There was nothing and no one whom I did not love at that

moment. . . . I stood on the veranda and watched the coolies as they tramped down the road. Their movements, their forms, their countenances seemed strangely wonderful to me, as if they were all moving like waves in the great ocean of the world. When one young man placed his hand upon the shoulder of another and passed laughingly by, it was a remarkable event to me. . . . I seemed to witness, in the wholeness of my vision, the movements of the body of all humanity, and to feel the beat of the music and the rhythm of a mystic dance.

When clouds of judgment and projection slip from our eyes, and the miraculous sheen of our fellow human travelers is finally perceived— the one in the many, the many in the one—a very high level of love unfolds. From the most inner center of spiritual awareness, the most ennobling love of all our loves emerges: the love we name "compassion." Agape. Empathy. Charity. Sacrificial, self-giving love.

Compassion for our "neighbor," the known or unknown person who lives on the wealthiest or most squalid street; in the mansion or meanest ghetto; in the northern, southern, eastern, or western parts of the world: This is the love that imitates most closely the love of God. This feeling for the so-called "unlovable," the world's scorned "untouchables," those burned by hardship beyond repair, this love gives occasion to Holy Spirit to enter history. As one of our century's finest theologians, Karl Rahner, wrote, "Our encounter with our neighbor in love must be recognized—not as one experience among others—but as the central act of human existence. Compassion integrates the whole personal content of experience." In the moment of loving our neighbor, we are loving the Divine.

MAY I BE A PROTECTOR

May I be a protector to those without protection,
A leader for those who journey,
And a boat, a bridge, a passage
For those desiring the further shore.

May the pain of every living creature
Be completely cleared away.
May I be the doctor and the medicine
And may I be the nurse
For all sick beings in the world
Until everyone is healed.

Just like space
And the great elements such as earth,
May I always support the life
Of all the boundless creatures.

And until they pass away from pain
May I always be the source of life
For all the realms of varied beings
That reach unto the ends of space.

The Buddhist Master, Shantideva; India, eighth century

In Your Household

Faithful Friend of all who have no other friend,
To You I hold them up in my heart:
Stray animals and humans
Homeless, homesick, heartsick,
longing, lost.
Please, send them some sign that You care;
Make me alert to their need;
Let each of us find our little corner
in Your Household.
Amen.

Brother David Steindl-Rast, United States, twentieth century

By the Power of This Practice

May all beings know happiness, and the root of happiness,
May all be free from sorrow, and the cause of sorrow,
May all never be separated from the happiness which is sorrowless,
And may all live in harmony, without too much attachment or too
    much aversion,
And live believing in the equality of all that lives.

Traditional Buddhist prayer

WALK THE SACRED WAY

Grandfather,
Look at our brokenness,
We know that in all creation
Only the human family
Has strayed from the Sacred Way.

We know that we are the ones
Who are divided
And we are the ones
Who must come back together
To walk in the Sacred Way.

Grandfather,
Sacred One,
Teach us love, compassion, and honour
That we may heal the earth
And heal each other.

Prayer of the Ojibwa (Chippewa) people;
Canada, traditional

THAT ALL MAY BE ONE

My prayer is not for them alone. I pray also for those who will
believe in me through their message, that all of them may be
one, my God, just as You are in me, and I am in You.

John 17:20-23

FOR AS LONG AS SPACE EXISTS

For as long as space exists
And sentient beings endure,
May I too remain,
To dispel the misery of the world.
The Buddhist Master, Shantideva; India, eighth century

A Priestly Blessing

May the Lord bless you and keep you,

May the Lord make his face to shine upon you and be gracious
    unto you,

May the Lord lift up his countenance upon you and give you peace.

Numbers 6:24-26

Wherever I Go

Wherever I go
I see You, Vithoba.
I see You by my side.
You still take me by the hand:
You still guide me,
Wherever I go.
And as I walk along,
I still lean on You,
and You bear my burden, Lord!
In everyone I see a friend, indeed!
Within me and outside I feel
Your Holy Presence, Lord.
Around me and above are
You.

Tukaram, the poet-saint of
Maharashtra, India, 1607-1694

BRIGID'S FEAST

I should like a great lake of finest ale
For the King of kings.
I should like a table of the choicest food
For the family of heaven.
Let the ale be made from the fruits of faith,
And the food be forgiving love.

I should welcome the poor to my feast,
For they are God's children.
I should welcome the sick to my feast,
For they are God's joy.
Let the poor sit with Jesus at the highest
    place,
And the sick dance with the angels.

God bless the poor,
God bless the sick,
And bless our human race.
God bless our food,
God bless our drink,
All homes, O God, embrace.

Anonymous, Ireland, first millennium

Into the Love of God

O Lord, let Your love dissolve my hard heart. Let Your love raise
me above myself. Let Your love reveal to me joy beyond
imagination. Let my soul exhaust itself by singing the praises of
Your love. Let me love You more than I love myself, and let me
love myself only for Your sake. And let me see Your love shining
in the hearts of all people, that I may love them as I love You.

Thomas à Kempis; Germany, c. 1380-1471

Prayer of a Dying Man

And though I behold a man hate me,
I will love him.
O God, Father, help me, Father!
O God, Creator, help me, Father!
And even though I behold a man hate me
I will love him.

The Dinka people of the Sudan; traditional

Urban Spirituality

Every mountain is a paean to God,
winter trees dark against an orange sky
are prayer lines etched into the evening,
and patiently meandering rivers tend weariness.

But back in the city,
a walk on concrete-coated soil
and tantalizing glimpses of green and sky
only frustrate the spirit
that has been sated at earth's breast.

Where are the city places that nourish the spirit?

The City answers:

In clustered children, an urban meadow flowers,
colorful and wild with swaying—
romp with them to see God.

In the urge to thrive, God's life-gift,
pulsing by grace in spite of evil and despair—
notice the lives that throb with hope.

In spirits joined across barriers
that divide the known from the Other—
motor into the Kingdom on a city bus.

But especially in the sound of sirens.

Sirens, intrusive as the Word,
wailing pain and death daily, hourly,
audible ashes marking city spirits.
reminders of mortality that prompt
the compassion that landscapes left out.

No urban liturgy is complete
without the kyrie of a siren.
Its shrill keening reminds worshipers
of the world outside the sanctuary
and broadens the benediction.

Sirens. Calls to prayer that hold the spirit in solidarity with those
who suffer instead of in denial.

Sirens. Announcing death but bringing life when they keep the
faithful on the caring edge where Jesus walked.

Margaret G. Payne, United States, twentieth century

FROM *The Sonnets to Orpheus*

Silent friend of many distances, feel
how your breath enlarges all of space.
Let your presence ring out like a bell
into the night. What feeds upon your face

grows mighty from the nourishment thus offered.
Move through transformation, out and in.
What is the deepest loss that you have suffered?
If drinking is bitter, change yourself to wine.

In this immeasurable darkness, be the power
that rounds your senses in their magic ring,
the sense of their mysterious encounter.

And if the earthly no longer knows your name,
whisper to the silent earth: I'm flowing.
To the flashing water say: I am.

Rainer Maria Rilke; Germany, 1875-1926
Translated by Stephen Mitchell

LOVING ONE ANOTHER

Loving one another with the charity of Christ, may the love you
   have in your hearts be shown outwardly in your deeds so that,
   compelled by such an example, you may always grow in love of
   God and in charity for one another.

Clare of Assisi; Italy, c. 1193–1253

GIVE ME THE POWER TO LOVE

. . . My God, give me the power to love!
The world needs me and is waiting for me.
Even though I still cannot believe in other people's love
   and even though I still cannot believe in your Love,
at least give me the courage to risk my life for others
   and for one other,
      so that others may not suffer like me. . . .

Michel Quoist; France, twentieth century

WE ARE ONE

This ritual is ONE
The food is ONE
We who offer the food are ONE
The fire of hunger is also ONE
All action is ONE
We who understand this are ONE

A Hindu blessing: India, traditional

ABOUND IN LOVE

May the Lord make you to increase and abound in love one toward
another, and toward all men and women, even as we do toward
you: to the end that God may establish your hearts unblamable
in holiness.

1 Thessalonians 3:11–13

A Cardiologist's Prayer for His Patients

Lord, keep us mindful of Your Presence in all things:

Allow a daily quiet time to listen, to act upon
    Your guidance in all matters.
    Our world is so busy; it is so easy
    to postpone this aspect of living.

Encourage regular exercise to keep the Body Temple
    in health. Excuses come easily: "I'm too tired."
    "It's raining." "I haven't the time."

Transfer all concerns of daily living on to Your
    loving care. Struggling "to take charge" is
    exhausting; we need Your support—
    the inner peace—that comes from trust
    and letting go.

Finally, lead us along the path to wholeness—in mind, body,
and spirit enabling us to fully celebrate the gift of life,
and be better equipped to look to the needs of others.

William F. Haynes, Jr.; United States, twentieth century

THE SOUL

I am a flame of fire, blazing with passionate love;

I am a spark of light, illuminating the deepest truth;

I am a rough ocean, heaving with righteous anger;

I am a calm lake, comforting the troubled breast;

I am a wild storm, raging at human sins;

I am a gentle breeze, blowing hope in the saddened heart;

I am dry dust, choking worldly pride;

I am wet earth, bearing rich fruits of grace.
From The Black Book of Camarthan; Wales, first millennium

To the Sun

Great Sun Power, I am praying for my people that they may be
    happy in the summer and that they may live through the cold of
    winter. Many are sick and in want. Pity them and let them
    survive. Grant that they may live long and have abundance. May
    we go through these ceremonies correctly, as you taught our
    forefathers to do in the days that are past. If we make mistakes,
    pity us. Help us, Mother Earth, for we depend upon your
    goodness. Let there be rain to water the prairies, that the grass
    may grow long and the berries be abundant.

O Morning Star! when you look down upon us, give us peace and
    refreshing sleep. Great Spirit! bless our children, friends, and
    visitors through a happy life. May our trails lie straight and level
    before us. Let us live to be old. We are all your children and ask
    these things with good hearts.

The Indians of the Great Plains; Native America, traditional

GOD TO ENFOLD ME

God to enfold me, God to surround me,
God in my speaking, God in my thinking.
God in my sleeping, God in my waking,
God in my watching, God in my hoping.
God in my life, God in my lips,
God in my soul, God in my heart.
God in my sufficing, God in my slumber,
God in mine ever-living soul, God in mine eternity.

Celtic oral tradition; collected in Scotland, nineteenth century

YOU HAVE LED ME SO TENDERLY

Lord, when I look upon my own life it seems you have led me so
carefully, so tenderly, you could have attended to no one else;
but when I see how wonderfully you have led the world and are
leading it, I am amazed that you have had time to attend to
such as I.

Augustine of Hippo; 354–430, North Africa

WHY DID YOU TELL ME TO LOVE?

Lord, why did you tell me to love all men, my brothers?
I have tried, but I come back to you, frightened . . .

Lord, I was so peaceful at home, I was so comfortably settled.
It was well furnished, and I felt cozy.
I was alone, I was at peace,
Sheltered from the wind and the rain, kept clean.
I would have stayed unsullied in my ivory tower.
But, Lord, you have discovered a breach in my defenses.
You have forced me to open my door.
Like a squall of rain in the face, the cry of men has awakened me;
Like a gale of wind a friendship has shaken me,
Stealing in like a shaft of light, your grace has disturbed me.
Rashly enough, I left my door ajar. Now, Lord, I am lost!
Outside, men were lying in wait for me.
I did not know they were so near; in this house, in this street,
    in this office; my neighbor, my colleague, my friend.
As soon as I started to open the door I saw them, with out-
    stretched hands, anxious eyes, longing hearts,
    like beggars on church steps.

The first came in, Lord. There was, after all, a bit of space
    in my heart.
I welcomed them. I would have cared for them and fondled them,
    my very own little lambs, my little flock.
You would have been pleased, Lord; I would have served and
    honored you in a proper, respectable way.

Until then, it was sensible. . . .

But the next ones, Lord, the other men—I had not seen them;
 they were hidden behind the first ones.

There were more of them. They were wretched; they overpowered
 me without warning.

We had to crowd in, I had to find room for them.

Now they have come from all over in successive waves, pushing
 one another, jostling one another.

They have come from all over town, from all parts of the country,
 of the world; numberless, inexhaustible.

They don't come alone any longer but in groups, bound one to
 another.

They come bending under heavy loads; loads of injustice, of
 resentment and hate, of suffering and sin. . . .

They drag the world behind them, with everything rusted,
 twisted, badly adjusted.

Lord, they hurt me! They are in the way, they are all over.

They are too hungry; they are consuming me!

I can't do anything any more; as they come in, they push the
 door, and the door opens wider. . . .

Ah, Lord! My door is wide open!

I can't stand it any more! It's too much! It's no kind of a life!
 What about my job?
 My family?
 My peace?
 My liberty?
 And me?

Ah, Lord! I have lost everything; I don't belong to myself
    any longer;
There's no more room for me at home.

Don't worry, God says, you have gained all,
While men came in to you,
I, your God,
Slipped in among them.

Michel Quoist, France, twentieth century

Let My Life Be Like the Rainbow

From the great rock I see it, the Daybreak Star, the sign of the
  dawning;
Above the mountain it rises and my heart dances.
Now the light comes, the light that makes me one with all life.
Like the tinamou I am, who sings in the dawn, who is humble with
  love,
Who walks in the circle of the greater love and the greater power.
Let me be like a ray of light, like a flower blazing with light,
Like the waterfall laughing with light, like the great tree also,
Mighty in its roots that split the rocks, mighty in its head that
  reaches the sky,
And its leaves catch the light and sing with the wind a song of the
  circle.

Let my life be like the rainbow, whose colors teach us unity;
Let me follow always the great circle, the roundness of power,
One with the moon and the sun, and the ripple of waters,
Following the sacred way of honor, a guide and protector to the
  weak,
A rock of strength in my word that shall say no evil, no life nor
  deception.

Guaymi oral tradition; Panama and Costa Rica

THE TASK YOU HAVE GIVEN ME

Most high and glorious God,
lighten the darkness of my heart
and give me sound faith,
firm hope
and perfect love.
Let me, Lord, have the right feelings
and knowledge,
rightly to carry out
the task you have given me.
Amen.

Francis of Assisi; Italy, 1182-1226

Chapter 6

Loving

in

Times

of

Suffering

*P*ain plunges like a sword through creation, cutting into the being of everything that is, heaping wound after wound on bodies, splintering minds, shattering souls like dying stars. Some part of the ancient law of love, of the flame and flow of things in the great good universe, allows suffering to take its course, to take its time, to go on and on, inexplicably, unfathomably, relentlessly. At least once in a lifetime, everyone will confront unwillingly the dark abyss of suffering, to find there is nowhere left to go, no refuge or solace or hiding place, no human hope of redemption or relief.

In one of the West's most noble writings about this impasse, Rainer Maria Rilke wrote:

I think I am passing through solid rock,
as the ore lies,
alone.
Everything is close to my face,
and everything close to my face is stone.

I don't have much knowledge yet in pain,
so this massive darkness makes me small.
You break in!
So Your great transformation will happen to me,
and my great grief cry will happen to You.

Staggering through a loneliness that feels like stone, the poet stays on the barren trail of grief, until he arrives at that place of interior dignity and integrity where the dark eyes of suffering must acknowledge the presence of God or be blinded, perhaps forever.

In the life of the spirit, such extreme inevitable affliction is seen as a "teaching," as life's harshest guide to Divine truth and love, to healing and hope. At such ultimate times, such moments of absolute limit, of boundedness—when nothing, not even the closest friend or the oldest addiction assuages the pain—there in the midst of total abandonment breathes the living God, the Divine and only source of liberating strength. A great Bengali poet gave voice to both the dilemma and its solution when he asked long ago: "How can you spend this night without your Lord?" Like an artist driven to seek a super-reality when simple reality no longer inspires, those who encounter incurable cosmic pain are driven to God, compelled to seek something beyond human strength.

PAIN'S INFINITE DESERT

In the driest whitest stretch
Of pain's infinite desert
I lost my sanity
And found this rose.

Jalal al-Din Rumi; Persia, 1207–1273
Version by Andrew Harvey

THE DEATH OF MAIRI

She died, like the ruddy clouds in the east at the break of day,
which are envied by the sun for their beauty as it rises in its
glory to darken them.

She died, like a glimpse of sunlight when the shadow races in
pursuit; she died, like a rainbow when the shower has fallen and
its glory is past.

She died, like snow which lies on the shore by the sea, when the
pitiless tide flows over it—oh whiteness!—and it did not enjoy it
for long.

She died, like the voice of the harp when it is sweetest and most
solemn; she died, like a lovely tale when the telling has barely
begun.

She died, like the gleam of the moon when the sailor is afraid in
the dark; she died, like a sweet dream when the sleeper is sad
that it has gone.

She died, at the beginning of her beauty; Heaven could not
dispense with her; she died, oh Mairi died, like the sun quenched
at its rising.

Evan Maccoll, Scotland, 1808-1898

Here I Am, Lord

Tonight, Lord, I am alone.
Little by little the sounds died down in the church,
The people went away,
And I came home,
Alone.
I passed people who were returning from a walk.
I went by the movie house that was disgorging its crowd.
I skirted café terraces where tired strollers were trying to prolong
   the pleasure of a Sunday holiday.
I bumped into youngsters, who will never be my own.
Here I am, Lord,
Alone.
The silence troubles me,
The solitude oppresses me. . . .

Michel Quoist, France, twentieth century
Translated by Agnes M. Forsythe and Anne Marie de Commaille

As the Rain Hides the Stars

As the rain hides the stars, as the autumn mist hides the hills, as
   the clouds veil the blue of the sky, so the dark happenings of my
   lot hide the shining of your face from me. Yet, if I may hold
   your hand in the darkness, it is enough. Since I know that,
   though I may stumble in my going, you do not fall.

Celtic oral tradition: England, Ireland, Scotland, Wales, first millennium

DEPRESSION

Just as day declines to evening, so often after some little pleasure
my heart declines into depression. Everything seems dull, every
action feels like a burden. If anyone speaks, I scarcely listen. If
anyone knocks, I scarcely hear. My heart is as hard as flint.
Then I go out into the field to meditate, to read the holy
Scriptures, and I write down my deepest thoughts as though in a
letter to You. And suddenly your grace, O Lord, shatters the
darkness with daylight, lifts the burden, relieves the tension.
Soon tears follow sighs, and heavenly joy floods over me again.

Aelred of Rievaulx; England, c. 1110-1167

LORD, IT IS TIME

Lord, it is time. The summer was very big.
Lay Thy shadow on the sundials,
and on the meadows let the winds go loose.

Command the last fruits that they shall be full,
give them another two more southerly days,
press them on to fulfillment and drive
the last sweetness into the heavy wine.

Who has no house will build him one no
    more.
Who is alone now, long will so remain,
will wake, read, write long letters
and will in the avenue to and fro
restlessly wander, when the leaves are blowing.

Rainer Maria Rilke; Germany, 1875-1926

BEAR US AGAIN IN OUR ETERNAL MOTHER

O God,
how long will You forget us in our misery?
Take us again as Your children,
and bear us again in our eternal mother.

Jacob Boehme; Germany, 1575-1624

Waking in a Nazi Prison

O God, early in the morning I cry to You.
Help me to pray, and to think only of You.
I cannot pray alone.

In me there is darkness,
But with You there is light.
I am lonely, but You never leave me.

I am feeble in heart, but You are always strong.
I am restless, but in You there is peace.
In me there is bitterness, but with You patience.
Your ways are beyond my understanding,
but You know the way for me.

Lord Jesus Christ,
You were poor and wretched,
You were a captive as I am,
Cut off from your friends as I am
You know all human distress.

You abide in me, in my isolation.
You do not forget me, but seek me out.
You desire that I should know and love You.
Lord, I hear your call and follow You.

Holy Spirit

Grant me the faith that will protect me from despair.

Pour into me such love for You and for all people,

that any hatred and bitterness will be blotted out.

Grant me the faith that will deliver me from fear.

Dietrich Bonhoeffer, Germany, 1906-1945

THE PRAYER OF THE TIGER

A long time ago
when the cloak that covered this world was completely green,
And the cloak that covered the world above was completely blue,
Tigers lived in peace with human beings;
And human beings lived in peace with tigers; and with all other
    creatures.
Of course, like us the tigers, men sometimes killed to eat;
But only to eat;
And we, the tigers, could pace up and down forests of brilliant
plants without fearing anything but the Big Tiger Above;

And then men started to prefer the green of money to the green
of the tree. They came and killed us; and they killed
our children; and they wore our skin over theirs; they peeled
us like an orange but without eating us; and some of them even
killed us because it amused them, just for a game.

And we the tigers know many more things than men believe;
Perhaps we know more things than human beings;
There are fewer and fewer of us; the water isn't good to drink
anymore; the little monkeys we used to eat sometimes aren't
there any longer because there are no more trees for them to
climb.

O Great Tiger and Great Tigress; Gaze down with mercy and help
Your children the tigers, and help Your children the human beings;
Tell them that the great forest is almost destroyed:

Tell them that things can still, still, be changed,
But they must change themselves first.
Help them; and help us; so that the babies of tigers and the
babies of human beings don't become a very ancient idea, a
very sweet and sad idea, like the idea that, a long time ago,
this world below was a vast garden.

Eryk Hanut; Denmark, twentieth century

AS I WATCH THE MOON

As I watch the moon
Shining on pain's myriad paths,
I know I am not
Alone involved in Autumn.

Oe No Chisato; Japan, c. 825
Translated by Kenneth Rexroth

Intemerata Dei Mater

Pure and stainless Mother of God,
Noble Virgin,
Whom thousands of angels crowd around
And hymn unceasingly,
Look down on us, we beg You,
If this our praise of You deserves it.

You know how terrible the destiny of exiles is
On the shores where we have been abandoned.

No peace can last without You;
No hope for any work can be fulfilled without You;
No safety for our homes can remain, or for our world;
Or shelter for any of our possessions
Of which You, O Queen, are the most precious.

Mother of God, watch always over all things
And with a glad smile, embolden the just;
Feed them Your sweet honey;
Seat them at all moments at the Feast of God.

We beg You, O Mother,
To compel Your son
To gaze on our misery with compassion.
This we know is within Your power;
We are so weary, Mother, and tormented.
Stretch out the hand of Your Divine Grace to us

And help us leave this terrible abyss
And come safely at last to your City of Peace.

Traditional Christian prayer
Translated by Andrew Harvey

WHAT THEN SHALL SEPARATE US?

What then shall separate us from the love of Christ?
Shall affliction or tribulation?
Shall persecution, or famine,
or nakedness, or peril or sword?
As it is written:
"We are put to death all the day long for Your sake;
For Your sake we are prepared like sheep for the slaughter."
Yet in all these things,
we are more than victorious through God who loves us.
For I am fully assured
that neither death nor life,
nor angels nor principalities,
nor things present nor things to come,
nor powers, nor height, nor depth,
nor anything else in all creation,
shall separate us from the love of God
in Christ Jesus Our Lord.

Romans 8:35-39

A Prayer for Help

O Father, Creator, God, I ask Your help!
I invoke You, O my Father,
To You, Father, I turn,
To You, my God, I turn,
O Father,
My Father, I pray to You.
To You, in the time of the bright new moon,
I address my plea.

The Dinka people of the Sudan; traditional

CARIBBEAN WOMAN'S PRAYER

Wake up Lord
brush de sunflakes from yuh eye
back de sky a while Lord
an hear dis mother-woman
on behalf of her pressure-down people

God de Mudder
God de Fadder
God de Sister
God de Brudder
God de Holy Fire

Ah don't need to tell yuh
how tings stan
cause right now you know
dat old lizard ah walk
lick land
an you know hoe de pickney belly lang
and you know how de fork ah hit stone
an tho it rain you know it really drought
an even now de man have start fuh count de wata he make

God de Mudder
God de Fadder
God de Sister
God de Brudder
God de Holy Fire

Give me faith

O Lord
you know we is ah people
of a proud an generous heart
and how it shame us bad
dat we kyant welcome friend or stranger
when eat time come around

You know is not we nature
to behave like yard fowl

You know dat is de politics
an de times
an de tricks
dat has reduced we to dis

An talking bout politics Lord
Ah hope you give de politicians dem
de courage to do what de have to do
an to mek dem see dat tings must grow
from within
an not from without
even as you suffer us not
to walk in de rags of doubt

Mek dem see dat de people
must be at de root of de heart

dat dis place ain't Uncle Sam backyard
Lord, look how Rodney and Bishop get blast

God de Mudder
God de Fadder
God de Sister
God de Brudder
God de Holy Fire

To cut a laang story short
I want to see de children
wake up happy to de sunrise
an food in de pot

I want to see dem stretch limb
an watch dem sleep pon good stomach
I want to see de loss of hope
everywhere replace
wid de win of living

I want to see de man an woman
being in they being

Yes Lord
Halleliuh, Lord!

All green tings an hibiscus praises Lord
Grace Nichols: Caribbean Islands, twentieth century

THE FLOWER

. . . And now in age I bud again,
After so many deaths I live and write;
I once more smell the dew and rain,
And relish versing: Oh my only light,
   It cannot be
   That I am he
On whom your tempests fell all night. . . .
     George Herbert; England, 1593-1623

DAY OF THE LION

We are tillers of a cold soil,
exiles in a harsh land,
Wondering what to do
till the lion comes.
We are singers of the sad songs,
dancers on the quicksand,
Wondering what to do
till the lion comes.

We are travellers on an old road
that seldom gives us rest,
Pressing toward the day of the lion.
We are wanderers in a wasteland,
a tapping in our chests,
Signals of the day of the lion.
There are flashes through the long wait,
glances at the landscape
Glimpses of the day of the lion.
There are footprints by the roadside,
tracks that the sun has dried;
May be the tracks of the lion.

There are kings from the east and west,
veterans of the long hard quest
Gathered for the day of the lion;
There are stories we have never heard

echoes of the single word
Spoken on the day of the lion.

Thomas Renaud, United States, twentieth century

You Hear Our Anguish

God in Heaven! Great is your presence in all the world. You bear
the weight of the stars and govern the forces of the world
through immense spaces. Numberless as the sands are those who
have life and being through you. And yet, you hear the cry of all
the creatures, and the cry of the man and woman whom you
have specially formed. You hear the cry of all men and women
without confusing our mixed voices and without distinguishing
one from another as though you played favorites. You hear not
only the voice of one who is responsible for others and prays to
you in their name. You hear not only the voice of one who prays
for loved ones. . . . You hear also the most anguished man and
woman, the most abandoned, the most solitary one—alone in
the desert, alone in the multitude. Even if the forgotten one is
separated from all others, and in the crowd has become
unknown—having ceased to be a person except on a list—you
know that person. You have not forgotten anyone. You
remember our names. You know us where we are, retired, hidden
in the desert, unseen in the crowd, alone in the multitude. And
if in the thick shadows of dread, in the prey of terrible thoughts,
we are abandoned, you hear that anguish, too.

Søren Kierkegaard, Denmark, 1813-1855

KOL NIDRE

Kol Nidre—chant of ages,
Chant of Israel, chant of sorrow,
Measuring off the throbbing heartbeats
Of a people bowed in anguish,
Crushed by tyrants, thwarted, broken,
Wandering ever—homeless, weary,
Generations set your motif
Out of trials, hopes and yearnings,
Added each its variations
To your theme and to your cadence.
Diverse lands and diverse eras
Poured their soul into your music.
When we listen with our hearts attuned,
We can hear the lamentations
Through time's corridor resounding.
We can see revealed before us
heroes, martyrs, saints, and scholars,
Loyal steadfast sons of Israel
Sanctifying God, their father.

A Jewish Prayer for Yom Kippur; traditional

The Grapes of My Body

The grapes of my body can only become wine
After the winemaker tramples me.
I surrender my spirit like grapes to his trampling
So my inmost heart can blaze with joy.

Jalal al-Din Rumi; Persia, 1207-1273

Lament

I would like to step out of my heart
and go walking beneath the enormous sky.
I would like to pray.
And surely of all the stars that perished
long ago,
one still exists.
I think that I know
which one it is—
which one at the end of its beam in the sky,
stands like a white city. . . .

Rainer Maria Rilke; Germany, 1875-1926

And thou shalt speak and say before the Lord thy God: "A wandering Aramean was my father, and he went down into Egypt and sojourned there, few in number, and he became there a nation, great, mighty, and populous. And the Egyptians dealt ill with us, and afflicted us, and laid upon us hard bondage. And we cried unto the Lord, the God of our fathers, and the Lord heard our voice, and saw our affliction, and our toil, and our oppression. And the Lord brought us forth out of Egypt with a mighty hand, and with an outstretched arm, and with great terribleness, and with signs, and with wonders. And God hath brought us into this place, and hath given us this land, a land flowing with milk and honey. And now, behold, I have brought forth the first of the fruit of the land, which Thou, O God, hast given me." And thou shalt set it down before the Lord thy God, and worship before the Lord thy God.

Jewish; traditional

GOD'S PROTECTION

At Tara today in this fateful hour
I place all heaven within its power
And the sun with its brightness
And the snow with its whiteness
And the fire with all the strength it hath,
And lightning with its rapid wrath,
And the winds with their swiftness along their path,
And the sea with its deepness,
And the earth with its starkness:
All these I place,
By God's almighty grace,
Between myself and the powers of darkness.

Attributed to St. Patrick; Ireland, c. 390–c. 461

WHY DO YOU HIDE YOURSELF?

Why, O my Own, my Life, my All, do you hide Yourself from
   me? . . .

Why does that Heart, whose fiery flames I have felt so often, which
   has beaten against my heart, which has made mine a thousand
   times leap for joy, why does it appear today to be unconscious of
   my need and of sufferings? . . .

Why is it that, living as I do beneath the burning rays of my
   Eucharistic Sun, everything around me is ice, indifference and
   pain?

Why, Love of my loves, my Heaven, my Life, Heart of my soul,
   why leave my soul to be immersed and lose itself in an ocean of
   suffering?

Concepcion Cabrera de Armida, Mexico, 1862-1957

GOD ALONE SUFFICES

Let nothing disturb you,
Let nothing dismay you.
All things pass.
God never changes.
Patience attains
all that it strives for.
Those who have God
find they lack nothing.
God alone suffices.

Teresa of Ávila; Spain,
1515–1582

IN MY SOLITUDE

I am alone
On the road I travel,
On the road you take me,
Drawing me on with a force
That exceeds all human demands.

I am alone
And I feel this solitude
Like a deeply open wound
In the depths of my being.
All those who surround me
Are only shadowy figures,
Vanishing furtively
At the sound of my appeal.
They flee and disappear
When I try to approach them
And the time is coming
When I will settle into this solitude
And it will be my lone companion.

I do not know from where
This solitude comes to me.
Does it come from you?
Is it the only road
Where I will discover you
And find at last your truth?
Or does it come from other men

Who refuse to give me love
And thus drive me deeper down
Into a life of cold indifference?
Or does it come from me
Repulsing other human beings
As I try to draw them to me?

I walk, O Lord, in solitude
And the silence resounds in my ears
More loudly than the shouts of men.
I walk, O Lord, in solitude,
Plunging deeper into it
As I journey on to you,
My Lord and God.

François Chagneau; France, twentieth century

THE LORD IS MY SHEPHERD

The Lord is my shepherd; I shall not want.
He maketh me to lie down in green pastures;
He leadeth me beside the still waters.
He restoreth my soul;
He guideth me in straight paths for His name's sake.
Yea, though I walk through the valley of the shadow of death,
I will fear no evil,
For Thou art with me;
Thy rod and Thy staff, they comfort me.
Thou preparest a table before me in the presence of mine enemies;
Thou has anointed my head with oil; my cup runneth over.
Surely goodness and mercy shall follow me all the days of my life;
And I shall dwell in the house of the Lord for ever.

Psalm 23

To Tsuigoa, the Ancestor

O Tsuigoa,
father of fathers,
Thou art our father.
Let the rain fall from storm clouds,
Let our herds live.
Let us live.
Alas, I am so weak,
I am thirsty, I am hungry.
Oh, could I but eat the fruit of the fields!
Art Thou not our father,
father of fathers,
O Tsuigoa?
O, could we but praise thee,
could we but show our gratefulness!
Thou, father of fathers,
thou, our Master,
O Tsuigoa!

The Khoi Khoi people, South Africa, traditional

Why Do You Continue to Test My Soul?

Mother! Mother! Mother!
Why do you continue to test my soul
   with the suffering of this provisional world?
What more can I dedicate, sacrifice, release?
But do whatever you will with me.
I will continue to accept the play of daily life
   as your most precious teaching,
never ceasing to sing
   "Kali, Kali, Kali." . . .

Ramprasad Sen; Bengal, 1718–1775
Translated by Lex Hixon

Darkness Is as Light

If I say, Surely the darkness shall cover me
Even the light shall be night about
   me . . .
still the dark is not darkness to you
the night is as bright
   as the day;
for darkness is as
   light to you.

Psalm 139:11-12

Prayer to the Deceased

My child you have toiled through life and come to the end of
suffering.

Now you have gone, gone to whatever kind of place it may be, the
place where all are shorn, the place we all go to, the place of no
lights and no windows, never again to return, to come back. You
will think no more of what lies here, of what lies behind you.

At the end of many days you went away and left your
children, your grandchildren; you left them orphaned, you left
them living. You will think no more of what may become of
them.

We will go and join you, we will go be with you at the end of many
days.

Aztec; Mexico, traditional

Chapter 7

In Praise

of the

Sacred:
Mystical
Love

hen the heart bursts open in praise, we know that we love something far beyond and greater than ourselves. Pure and joyful, vibrant and radiant, moments of spontaneous praise express the most refined emotion of which men and women are capable: Gratitude. Thankfulness. Appreciation.

Emanating from the highest octaves of the human spirit, praise acknowledges humanity's timeless experience of a luminous presence within and at work in the world. In every society and century, immense stores of poetry, songs, hymns, prayers, and chants of praise record the rapture of the spirit when one reaches out toward the Infinite and finds at one's fingertips an ocean of holy light.

When the brilliant English poet, Christopher Smart, who called the Psalms "the Great Book of Gratitude," lay close to death in debtor's prison, he was writing in *Jubilate Agno* great lists of objects for which he felt gratitude: for Geoffrey, his cat, "the servant of the living God" who "purrs in thankfulness"; for nutmeg and lightning; for the letters of the alphabet, the beginning of learning; for colors, which are "spiritual"; "for the blessing of God upon the grass in shades of green"; for the man on the corner who had lent him money; for sunshine that illumines the air with brightness every day; for the mystery in numbers; and for all that grows under the moist light of the moon.

Despite unimaginable suffering—betrayal, loss, sickness, starvation, total abandonment—it was Smart's instinctive reaction to the gift of life to praise, thank, worship, appreciate, be grateful for whatever he experienced. As long as he lived and breathed, his huge heart echoed the pulse of cosmic love, returning to life with every beat a "thank you" for that which is.

Few writings capture humanity's sense of gratitude more regally than the magnificent "Canticle of the Creatures" by one of the world's true masters of praise, Francis of Assisi:

> . . . Praise be to you, my Lord, for all your Creatures, above all, Brother Sun, who gives us the light of day. For he is beautiful, and radiant with great splendour. . . .
> Praise be to You, my Lord, for Sister Moon and the stars. In heaven You fashioned them, clear and precious and beautiful.
> Praise be to You, my Lord, for Brother Wind, and for every kind of weather, cloudy or fair, stormy or serene, by which You cherish all that You have made.
> Praise be to You, my Lord, for Sister Water, which is useful and humble and precious and pure.
> Praise be to You, my Lord, for Brother Fire, by whom You lighten the night, for he is beautiful and playful and robust and strong.

In this Canticle lies the only possible answer to the perennial question: What do the mystics mean when they say that they love "God"? What do *we* mean when we say that we love "God"? We love the flowing light of the sun and moon and stars. We love the ancient wandering river of the Tao. The sea of grace that saturates the soul with the vivid aromas and colors of things. The uncreated current flowing on and on endlessly throughout creation. We love the lover, the beloved, and love itself.

I Am Giving You Love with My Whole Heart

I am giving You worship with my whole life,
I am giving You assent with my whole power,
I am giving You praise with my whole tongue,
I am giving You honor with my whole utterance.
I am giving You kneeling with my whole desire,
I am giving You love with my whole heart,
I am giving You my soul, O God of Gods.

Celtic oral tradition: England, Ireland, Scotland, and Wales,
first millennium

Praise be to You, my Lord, for all your Creatures, above all, Brother Sun, who gives us the light of day. For he is beautiful, and radiant with great splendour, and so is like You, most high Lord.

Praise be to You, my Lord, for Sister Moon and the stars. In heaven You fashioned them, clear and precious and beautiful.

Praise be to You, my Lord, for Brother Wind, and for every kind of weather, cloudy or fair, stormy or serene, by which You cherish all that You have made.

Praise be to You, my Lord, for Sister Water, which is useful and humble and precious and pure.

Praise be to You, my Lord, for Brother Fire, by whom You lighten the night, for he is beautiful and playful and robust and strong.

Praise be to You, my Lord, for our Sister Earth, who sustains and governs us, and produces varied fruits with colored flowers and herbs.

Praise be to You, my Lord, for those who are forgiving in Your love, and for those who bear sickness and tribulation. . . .

Praise be to You, my Lord, for our sister, Bodily Death, from whom no living person can escape. . . .

Blessed are those who in death are close to You, for death shall do them no harm.

Praise and bless my Lord, giving thanks, and serving others with great humility. . . .

Francis of Assisi; Italy, 1182–1226

The Full Four Seasons

O Lord of Creation, O Word-Made-Flesh, incarnating yourself in all the matter of the universe, you are not merely summer to my soul, but the full four seasons.

I love you in the sensuousness of summer, when leaves wax green and the garden is a riot of color and joy, when your sun kisses my bare skin and cool water laves every part of my body.

I love you in the magic and melancholy of autumn, when your earth-body dies in a blood-red blaze of glory and something in me saddens and dies, too, as I come to terms with change, mortality, and ephemerality.

I love you in the dead of winter, when the wind howls over the brown and barren earth outside the window and inside my soul, when the heart can freeze like snow and ice or rest easy, asleep like the garden, waiting patiently for your beneficent touch of spring.

I love you in the lush burgeoning of springtime, when new life bursts from the womb of earth as you burst from the stone-cold tomb and rose from the dead on Easter.

You are every season to my soul: summer, fall, winter, and spring. You are the four seasons all at once. And you transcend them all in a timeless time beyond both earth and our wildest imaginings of heaven.

May I not sleepwalk but stay fully awake through the full four
seasons of the year and never miss the slightest nuance of your
vast overture of love for me and all of creation. Amen.

Tessa Bielecki; United States, twentieth century

I gird myself today with the might of heaven.
The rays of the sun,
The beams of the moon,
The glory of fire,
The speed of wind,
The depth of sea,
The stability of earth,
The hardness of rock,
I gird myself today with the power of
   God:
God's strength to comfort me,
God's might to uphold me,
God's wisdom to guide me,
God's eye to look before me,
God's ear to hear me,
God's word to speak for me,
God's hand to lead me,
God's way to lie before me,
God's shield to protect me,
God's angels to save me
From the snares of the devil,
From temptations to sin,
From all who wish me ill,
Both far and near,
Alone and with others.

     Attributed to St. Patrick; Ireland, c. 390-c. 461

All Living Things Bless and Praise You

O Lord,
creator of all the world
all living things
bless and praise you.

Jewish, traditional

Searching for God

O Lord my God, teach my heart today where to see you, how to see you, where and how to find you. You have made me and remade me, and you have given me all the good things I have ever possessed—and still I do not know you.

Teach me to seek you, for I cannot seek you unless you teach me, or find you unless you reveal yourself to me.

Help me to seek you in desire, help me desire you in my seeking, help me to find you by loving you, help me to love you when I find you.

St. Anselm of Canterbury, England, 1033–1109

NOTHING IS ENOUGH

If my lips could sing as many songs
as there are waves in the sea:
if my tongue could sing as many hymns
as there are ocean billows:
if my mouth
filled the whole firmament with praise:
if my face
shone like the sun and moon together:
if my hands
were to hover in the sky like powerful eagles
and my feet
ran across mountains as swiftly as the deer;
all that would not be enough
to pay you fitting tribute,
O Lord my God.

Jewish hymn: Talmudic era, third to fifth century

LORD OF MY HEART

Lord of My Heart, give me vision to inspire me, that, working or
   resting, I may always think of You.

Lord of My Heart, give me light to guide me, that at home or
   abroad, I may always walk in Your way.

Lord of my heart, give me wisdom to direct me, that, thinking or
   acting, I may always discern right from wrong.

Lord of my heart, give me courage to strengthen me, that, amongst
   friends or enemies, I may always proclaim Your justice.

Lord of my heart, give me trust to console me, that, hungry or
   well-fed, I may always rely on Your mercy.

Lord of my heart, save me from empty praise, that I may always
   boast of You.

Lord of my heart, save me from worldly wealth, that I may always
   look to the riches of heaven.

Lord of my heart, save me from military prowess, that I may always
   seek Your protection.

Lord of my heart, save me from vain knowledge, that I may always
   study Your word.

Lord of my heart, save me from unhealthy pleasures, that I may
   always find joy in Your beautiful creation.

Lord of my heart, whatever may befall me, rule over my thoughts
   and feelings, my words and actions.

Celtic oral tradition; England, Ireland, Scotland, and Wales, first millennium

Lost in You

The world is filled with you, yet you are not in it:
All are lost in you, but you are not within them.
The world is filled with your name, but of you there is no trace.
Their minds have been opened, but you they see not.
The world of the mind and of the soul was astounded,
For you remained hidden behind such a curtain.
O Pure One, I speak from my own helplessness:
You are both known and knower: what knowledge do I have?

Sherafuddin Maneri; North East India, thirteenth century

Alone with You

O my Lord,
the stars glitter
and the eyes of men are closed.
Kings have locked their doors
and each lover is alone with his love.

Here, I am alone with You.

Rabia; today's Iraq, 717-801

Where Thou Art, There Is Heaven

My Lord God, my All in All, Life of my life, Spirit of my spirit,
look in mercy upon me and so fill me with Your Holy Spirit
that my heart shall have no room for love of aught but You.

I seek from You no other gift but Yourself who are the giver of life
and all its blessings. From You I ask not for the world or its
treasures, nor yet for heaven even make request, but You alone
do I desire and long for, and where You are, there is heaven. The
hunger and the thirst of this heart of mine can be satisfied only
with You who have given me birth.

O my Creator! You have created my heart for Yourself alone, and
not for another. Therefore this my heart can find no rest or ease
save in You, in You who have both created it and set in it this
very longing for rest. Take away then from my heart all that is
opposed to You, and enter and abide and rule forever.

Sadhu Sundar Singh; India, 1889-c. 1929

MAY YOUR KINGDOM COME

O God,
grant that your kingdom may come this day
while we yet live.
Let this be brought to pass. Amen.
May your ineffable name
be praised, blessed, and exalted,
although it is far above all human speech and blessing,
far above all words that come from human lips.
May this be brought to pass. Amen.

From a Jewish prayer composed during the time of the Second Temple,
c. 516 B.C.-70 A.D.

ALL NIGHT I COULD NOT SLEEP

All night I could not sleep
because of the moonlight on my bed.
I kept on hearing a voice calling:
Out of Nowhere, Nothing answered "yes."

From the Ei Yfe folk song collection; China,
sixth to third century B.C.
Translated by Arthur Waley

YOU ARE GOD

You are the peace of all things calm
You are the place to hide from harm
You are the light that shines in dark
You are the heart's eternal spark
You are the door that's open wide
You are the guest who waits inside
You are the stranger at the door
You are the calling of the poor
You are my Lord and with me still
You are my love, keep me from ill
You are the light, the truth, the way
You are my Saviour this very day.

*Celtic oral tradition: England, Ireland,
Scotland, Wales, first millennium*

May My Soul Always Rove Around You

May your savour and your sweetness fill my soul! May it always thirst for you, O fountain of life, O fountain of wisdom, O fountain of knowledge, O fountain of eternal light, O torrent of desire and fertility in the mansion of God! May my soul always rove around you, and seek you and find you! Let it turn to you and come to you! May you be the object of its thought and of its word. Let it sing your praise and the glory of your beloved name with humility and reserve, with love and delight, with ease and tenderness, with patience and peace, with success and perseverance unto the very end. You alone shall be all in all to me, you shall always be my hope, my confidence, my riches, my charm, my pleasure, my delight, my repose, my tranquillity, my peace, my suavity, my perfume, my sweetness, my refreshment, my nurture, my love, my thought, my support, my desire, my refuge, my succour, my patience, my treasure, my passion! My spirit and my heart shall always be fixed and locked and deeply rooted in you, and in you only! Amen.

St. Bonaventure; Italy, 1221–1274

Are You Not Water Itself?

Tell me, Lord, how indeed
may I offer worship to You.
Do You ask me, Lord,
to give oblation of water to You?
Are You not water itself?
Do You ask me to offer flowers to You?
The fragrance of the flowers, too, are You?
And how may I sing to You?
Are You not the song Yourself?
Do I in kirtan use the symbols which I love?
These, too, are You not Yourself?
Where is the ground on which I may stand
And dance to You?
Are You not every inch of space?
Wherever I turn, I behold Your face.

Tukaram, the poet-saint of Maharashtra, India,
1607–1694

O eternal God, fire and abyss of charity, . . . I have tasted and
seen your depth, eternal Trinity, and the beauty of your creation.
. . . O abyss! O eternal Godhead! O deep sea! What more
could you have given me than the gift of your very self? . . .
You are a fire lifting all chill and giving light. In your light you
have made me know your truth . . . Good above every good,
joyous Good, Good beyond measure and understanding! Beauty
above all beauty . . . You who are the angels' good are given to
humans with burning love. You, garment who covers all shame,
pasture the starving within your sweetness, for you are sweet
without trace of bitterness.

Catherine of Siena; Italy, 1347-1380

What Is the Divine Darkness?

Supernal Triad, Deity above all essence, knowledge and goodness;
Guide of Souls to Divine Wisdom; direct our path to the
ultimate summit of Thy mystical Lore, most incomprehensible,
most luminous, and most exalted, where the pure, absolute, and
immutable mysteries of theology are veiled in the dazzling
obscurity of the secret Silence, outshining all brilliance with the
intensity of their Darkness, and surcharging our blinded
intellects with the utterly impalpable and invisible fairness of
glories surpassing all beauty.

Let this be my prayer; but do thou, dear Timothy, in the diligent
exercise of mystical contemplation, leave behind the senses and
the operations of the intellect, and all things sensible and
intellectual, and all things in the world of being and non-being,
that thou mayest arise, by unknowing, towards the union, as far
as is attainable, with The One Who transcends all being and all
knowledge. For by the unceasing and absolute renunciation of
thyself and of all things, thou mayest be borne on high, through
pure and entire self-abnegation, into the superessential Radiance
of the Divine Darkness.

Pseudo-Dionysius; Syria, c. 500

Praise Ye the Lord

Praise the Lord. Praise the Lord, O my soul.
While I live will I praise the Lord: I will sing
praises unto my God while I have any being.

Psalm 146:1-2

O My Beloved Star

O my beloved Star,
so fascinate me
that I may not withdraw from Your radiance.

O consuming Fire,
Spirit of Love,
"come upon me,"
and create in my soul an incarnation of your Word.

Elizabeth of the Trinity, France, 1880-1906

LET EVERYTHING THAT BREATHES PRAISE GOD

Hallelujah.
Praise God in His sanctuary;
Praise Him in the sky, His stronghold . . .
Praise Him with blasts of the horn;
Praise Him with harp and lyre.
Praise Him with timbrel and dance;
Praise Him with resounding cymbals;
Praise Him with loud-clashing cymbals.
Let everything that breathes praise God.

Psalm 150

Why Do You Stay in the World?

O heart, why do you lie bound in this transient world? Fly out
from this cramped space, for you are a bird that belongs to the
world of spirits. You are a friend that would always be alone, with
the beloved, abiding behind the veil of mystery. Why do you stay
in this world, which is passing away? Consider what state you are
in, escape from your captivity in this material world and go forth
to the grassy lawns of spiritual reality. You belong to the Divine
world, you would be welcome in the assembly of Love: it would
be grievous for you to remain in this abode. Each morning there
comes a voice from heaven calling: "You will find the road clear
for passage, when you make the dust to lie on it." On the way
to the *Ka'ba* of union with Him, you will see at the root of every
thorn, thousands who gave up their young lives for the sake of
love. Thousands fell wounded on this road and there did not
come to them any breath of the fragrance of union, or sign from
the abode of the Beloved.

Jalal al-Din Rumi; Persia, 1207–1273

I Want to Love You

Lord, I want to love you, yet I'm not sure.

I want to trust you, yet I'm afraid of being taken in.

I know I need you, yet I'm ashamed of the need.

I want to pray, yet I'm afraid of being a hypocrite.

I need my independence, yet I fear to be alone.

I want to belong, yet I must be myself.

Take me, Lord, yet leave me alone.

Lord, I believe; help thou my unbelief.

O Lord, if you are there, you do understand, don't you?

Give me what I need but leave me free to choose.

Help me work it out my own way, but don't let me go.

Let me understand myself, but don't let me despair.

Come unto me, O Lord—I want you there.

Lighten my darkness—but don't dazzle me.

Help me to see what I need to do and give me strength to do it.

O Lord, I believe; help thou my unbelief.

Bernard, S.S.F., England, twentieth century

That prayer has the greatest power
which you make with all your might.
It makes a bitter heart grow sweet,
A sad heart merry,
A poor heart rich,
A foolish heart wise,
A timid heart brave,
A sick heart well,
A blind heart full of sight,
A cold heart fervent.
It draws the great God down to the little heart,
It drives the thirsty soul up to the fullness of God.
It brings together two lovers,
God and the soul,
In a wondrous place where they speak much of love.

Mechthild of Magdeburg: Germany. c. 1212–c. 1280

You Are Fire

You are fire, but Your fire is veiled, for in all to which You have
joined Yourself, You are under a veil. You are the Breath of Life
in both body and soul. You are the water of Life to be found in
every place. In every form You manifest Yourself, according to
Your will; even in the dust are Your mysteries shown forth; You
are the mine and show Yourself in its jewels. You, the Creator,
are seen in the creatures, Spirit shining through gross matter.

You are God in Absolute Unity and You dwell here in body and
soul, for You are the Divine Essence dwelling in the midst of
each one of us. O Lord Most High, how glorious is the
manifestation of Your Light! You are the Sought and the
Seeker: what remains to be said? Give me, I pray You, to drink
from the cup of Immortality, for You are the Cup and the Wine
and Cup-bearer.

Farid al-Din 'Attar; Persia, d. c. 1229

When I Love You

O Incomprehensible One, when I love You, when I break out of
the narrow circle of myself and leave behind the restless agony of
unanswered questions, when my blinded eyes no longer look
merely from afar and from the outside upon Your
unapproachable brilliance, and much more when You Yourself
have become through love the inmost center of my life, then I
can bury myself entirely in You. And with myself, all my
questions and doubts, O Mysterious God.

Karl Rahner; Germany, 1904-1984

It Is Right to Give Thanks

It is meet and right, it is expedient for our souls and bodies, eternal
Master, Lord God the Father Almighty, at all times and in all
places, to praise you, to hymn you, to bless you, to serve you, to
adore you, to give thanks to you, to glorify you, to confess to
you, with unsilenced heart and unwearied doxologies. You are the
one who made the heavens and the things that are in the
heavens, the earth and all things that are therein. You are the
one who made man and woman after your own image, and made
all things through your wisdom. For these things we give thanks
from the rising of the sun to the going down of the sun, and
from the north to the south, through Jesus Christ our Lord.
Amen.

Coptic Liturgy of St. Mark; Egypt, first century, formulated
eighteenth to nineteenth century

HASIDIC SONG

Wherever I go—only You! Wherever I stand—
only You! Just You; again You; always You!

Jewish; traditional

O GIVER OF MINDS AND SOULS

O my God, Lord of all that exists, of all intellectual beings and all
sensible things, O Giver of minds and souls, Who laid the
foundations of the world, First Cause of all existence and
Dispenser of all bounty, You Maker of hearts and spirits and
Fashioner of forms and bodies, O Light of lights and ruler of all
the spheres, You are the First, there was none before You; You
are the Last, there shall be none after You. The angels are not
able to comprehend Your Majesty, and people cannot attain to a
knowledge of the perfection of Your Essence. O God, set us free
from the things that bind us, and deliver us from all evil that
may hinder us. Send down upon our spirits Your gracious
influence and shed forth upon our souls the bright beams of
Your Light. The mind is but one drop in the ocean of Your
Kingdom and the soul is but a spark of Your Divine Glory.
Praise be to You Whom the sight cannot perceive, or can the
thought conceive of Your likeness: to You be thanksgiving and
praise. You give and You take away: You are the All-Bountiful
and the All-Abiding. Praise be to You, for Yours is the power
over all things and unto You shall we return.

Suhrawardi Halabi; Persia, d. 1191

Chapter 8

Divine
Love

in

Everyone

and

Everything

*T*here are no words beautiful enough to describe the soul's experience of God's love. A mystery beyond all other mysteries, a feeling far beyond all other feelings, a light truly incomprehensible to the intellect, Divine love cannot be directly conveyed in human words. Throughout history, people with spiritual awareness, confronting the almost unbearable beauty of The Holy One, have invoked the sacred language of symbols to share what they have experienced. In spiritual traditions as diverse as the Maya, Sufi, Bengali, or Hasidic, in order to express the true "otherness" of the holy, authors have created symbols from the most majestic and lovely aspects of nature, as in the ancient Celtic prayer, "I Am," a lyric of images strung like pearls on a silver thread:

> . . . I am the beam of the moon and the stars,
> I am the power of trees growing,
> I am the bud breaking into blossom,
> I am the movement of the salmon swimming,
> I am the courage of the wild boar fighting.
> I am the speed of the stag running.

The twelfth-century visionary, Hildegard of Bingen, also used radiant images drawn from nature to convey her experience of the divine in every being and atom and cell. She named this holy energy "The Living Light":

I, the fiery life of Divine essence, am aflame beyond the beauty
   of the meadows. I gleam in the waters. I burn in the sun,
   moon and stars. With every breeze, as with invisible life that
   embraces everything, I awaken all creatures to life. . . .

I am the breeze that nurtures all things green. I encourage
   blossoms to flourish with ripening fruits,
I am the rain coming from the dew that causes the grasses to
   laugh with the joy of life. . . .

Poet-saints and sages from all over the world have left images of
deifying energies streaming down like waterfalls from the heavens
onto earth, infusing men and women with immeasurably holy love.
Such images reveal how uncreated love sparks every creature with life,
moistens the soul with grace, and circulates in the being of everyone
and everything, increasing without limits the human capacity to love.
Divine Love is often portrayed like a mother hugging her child, encir-
cling, sheltering, comforting, holding, and keeping it warm in an em-
brace that cannot end.

Today, as much of what is soulless in the West collapses, as a
scientific perception of life recedes into the background of human
consciousness, our collective experience of the Divine moves into the
foreground; the horizon of history abounds with hope and with rea-
sons to trust in the sacred promises made in wisdom literature. Eter-
nal love flows like a river of light throughout the universe. The Holy
One is in our midst, within us and among us. All suffering ends in
grace. All sorrow dissolves in the sweetness, beauty, tenderness, and
radiance of eternal love.

Because God Loves It

God showed me in my palm
A little thing round as a ball
About the size of a hazelnut.

I looked at it with the eye of understanding
And asked myself:
"What is this thing?"
And I was answered: "It is everything that is created."

I wondered how it could survive since it seemed so little
It could suddenly disintegrate into nothing.

The answer came: "It endures and ever will endure,
Because God loves it."

And so everything has being
Because of God's love.

Julian of Norwich; England, c. 1342-c. 1413

O Kali, the drama of my life
   was composed and acted out
in the blazing summer field of destiny.

Now please bring Your small child home
   through the fragrant cool of evening,
cradled in Your arms, lost in Your gaze,
   disappearing in Your love. . . .

       Ramprasad Sen, Bengal, 1718–1775
         Translated by Lex Hixon

What Gift Can I Offer You?

Mother of Infinity,
what gift can I offer you?
Plunging deep into meditation,
I perceive all lives and worlds are yours alone.
Why should your lovers present you
    with necklaces of gems and garments of
    silk?
The universe is a boundless ocean of jewels
    that humbly touches your feet,
the blackness between stars your only
    covering.
You are the mountain of inexhaustible
    abundance.
You reign over the golden city of truth.
Compared with your divine wealth,
even the Absolute appears as a wandering
    beggar
    clothed only in open space. . . .

Ramprasad Sen; Bengal, 1718-1775
Translated by Lex Hixon

EVERYTHING COMES FROM YOU

Everything comes from You, O Lord, and we have given You only
what comes from Your hand. We are foreigners and strangers in
Your sight, as were our ancestors. Our days on earth are but a
shadow, without hope. As for all this abundance that we have
provided for building You a temple for Your holy name, it comes
from Your hand, and all of it belongs to You, O Lord our God.
I know, my God, that You test the heart and are pleased with
integrity. All these things have I given willingly and with honest
intent. And now I have seen with joy how willingly Your people
have given to You, O Lord, our God, God of our fathers,
Abraham, Isaac and Israel.

1 Chronicles 29:14-17

I AM MUSTAFAH THE TAILOR

O God, I am Mustafah the tailor and I work at the shop of
Muhammad Ali. The whole day long I sit and pull the needle
and the thread through the cloth. O God, you are the needle
and I am the thread. I am attached to you and I follow you.
When the thread tries to slip away from the needle it becomes
tangled and must be cut so that it can be put back in the right
place. O God, help me to follow you wherever you may lead me.
For I am really only Mustafah the tailor, and I work at the shop
of Muhammad Ali on the great square.

Muslim; source unknown

Hear Me

Hear me, four quarters of the world—
a relative I am!
Give me the strength to walk the soft earth,
a relative to all that is.
Give me the eyes to see
and the strength to understand
that I may be like you.
With your power only can I face the winds.
Black Elk; Oglala Sioux, twentieth century

You Alone Arouse My Love

O, Lord,
I am overwhelmed by Your love. I am overwhelmed by Your
presence at my side. My soul by itself knows nothing of love, and
You alone arouse my love.

I feel I am drinking the sweetest wine, and drunk with love for You,
I will obey Your slightest wish. I could even lay down my life for
You.

Now that I know Your presence, all other pleasures in the world are
worthless. My only joy is to be with You.
Mechthild of Magdeburg; Germany, c. 1212–c. 1280

You Have Made Us for Yourself

How great You are, O Lord, and how greatly to be praised! How
incomparable is Your power and how infinite Your
understanding. We may be but a speck in Your vast creation, but
we want to praise You. We may carry around with us our
mortality and our sin as mute testimony to the truth that "God
resists the proud," but even so we want to praise Your name.
You have thrilled us by giving us delight in Your praise. You have
made us for Yourself, O Lord, and our hearts are restless until
they rest in You.

Augustine of Hippo, North Africa, 354-430

Sea and Rivers

O God, whose love is without measure: out of the depths of my
own creatureliness and yearning I call to you. Out of your own
depths of power and mystery you call to me. Enable me to enter
into the beginnings of the secrets of your love, and let the poor
stream of my life flow into the immensity of your being.

Brother Ramon; England, twentieth century

A SIKH PRAYER

O Lord, my heart is full of gratitude for Your various gifts and
blessings. The gratitude of heart and lips alone is insufficient
until I devote myself to Your service with my life and prove it by
my deeds. To You be thanks and praise for bringing me . . .
out of non-being into being, and for making me glad in Your
love and fellowship. I do not know You fully, and do not even
know my own needs: but You, O God, know well Your creatures
and their needs. I am not able to love myself as much as You
love me. In reality, to love oneself means that I should love with
heart and soul the boundless love which created me and which is
Yourself. It is for this very reason that You have created in me
only one heart, that it should be joined only to One, to You who
created it.

Sadhu Sundar Singh; India, 1889–c. 1929

BLESSING

O Lord, Creator
of all the world,
all living things
bless you!
Jewish; traditional

You Have Welcomed Me

Lord, because I am the lowliest of creatures,
You have raised me to Yourself.

Lord, because I have no earthly treasures,
You have poured upon me heavenly wealth.

Lord, because I am dressed in the grey rags of flaws,
You have clothed me in the pure white robe of grace.

Lord, because I desire the merest hut for my home,
You have welcomed me to Your eternal palace.

Mechthild of Magdeburg, Germany, c. 1212–c. 1280

Vanishing into Love

When the mystery of love is unveiled to you
You exist no longer, but vanish into love.
Place before the Sun a burning candle,
You will see its brilliance disappear before that blaze,
The candle is no longer, it is Light.
There are no more signs of it;
It has become a sign.

Jalal al-Din Rumi, Persia, 1207–1273

I thank You, O my light, eternal light, never failing light! You, the
highest and most immutable good!
I thank You! Now I can see. I see the light that shines in the
darkness.

And what do you see in this light?

I see how greatly You love me and that, if I remain in You, it is
just as impossible that You should not love me at all times, and
in all places, and in all ways, as that I should ever not love You.

Gerlach Peters; Holland, 1378-1411

Let the Whole Creation Praise You

Let the whole creation praise You, O Lord of
the world! Oh, that a voice might go forth over all the
earth, proclaiming Your faithfulness to those who love
You! All things fail; but You, Lord of all, never fail! They
who love You, oh, how little they have
to suffer! Oh, how gently, how tenderly, how sweetly
You, O my Lord, deal with them! Oh, that no
one had ever been occupied with any other love than
Yours! It seems as if You subjected those who
love You to a severe trial: but it is in order that they
may learn, in the depths of that trial, the depths of
Your love, O my God. Oh, that I had understanding
and learning, and a new language, in order to
magnify Your works, according to the knowledge of
them which my soul possesses! Everything fails me,
O my Lord; but if You will not abandon me, I will
never fail You. Let all the learned rise up against me,
let the whole creation persecute me, let the evil spirits
torment me—but You, O Lord, fail me not; for
I know by experience now the blessedness of that
liberation which You effect for those who
trust only in You.

Teresa of Avila; Spain, 1515-1582

I Am the Breeze

I am the one whose praise
echoes on high.

I adorn all the earth.

I am the breeze
that nurtures all things
green.
I encourage blossoms to flourish with ripening fruits.
I am led by the spirit to feed
the purest streams.

I am the rain
coming from the dew
that causes the grasses to laugh
with the joy of life.

I call forth tears,
the aroma of holy work.

I am the yearning for good.

Hildegard of Bingen: Germany. 1098-1179

Oh Trinity, restore in each of us your Image and Likeness of
Divine Love, and perfect us in your holiness, that wise,
compassionate affection. Purify our minds and wills of poisonous
cynicism, despair, inertia, and ignorance. Let us leave behind all
egotism, self-seeking and sin.

Envelop us with your Divine Presence.
Invade our inner being. Flood us with your
vital energy, your deifying grace, your
very spiritual substance.

Refashion us, transforming us into that very Love you yourself are,
and we are called to be.

Communicate your inner life to us in the intimacy of mystical
union, in that intense flow of Divine Love that raises each of us
to supreme identity in you, having healed our wounds and
removed every obstacle within us.

Fuse all our faculties together in the act of loving you in your
Eternal Now. Then let your vitality, your energizing and
sanctifying grace be our constant nourishment.

Let us become icons of your infinite compassion
for a world torn by ignorance, hate, greed and selfishness.

Cultivate in us that lucid awareness Divine Love is, and permit it
to bear fruit in our thoughts, attitudes, words, and actions as

that sublime and precious sensitivity that is the very heart of
your Godhead.

May we spread your sensitivity, your boundless caringness
everywhere, live it into being wherever we are, and never cease to
see and to be.

Wayne Teasdale; United States, twentieth century

TRIED BY THE TEMPEST

To those who are tried by the tempest, You are the calm harbour;
You are the object of all hope.

To those who are sick, You are their health; You guide the blind
and give help to those in need.

To those who face suffering, You always grant grace. You are
a light in darkness, a place of rest for the weary.

Severus of Thrace; Heraclea, d. c. 304

What Is That Light?

What is that light which shines upon me but not continuously, and
   strikes upon my heart with no wounding? I draw back in terror:
   I am on fire with longing: terror insofar as I am different from
   it, longing in the degree of my likeness to it. It is Wisdom,
   Wisdom itself, which in those moments shines on me, cleaving
   through my cloud. And the cloud returns to wrap me round once
   more as my strength is beaten down under its darkness and the
   weight of my sadness: for my strength is weakened through
   poverty, so that I can no longer support my good, until You,
   Lord, who are merciful to me, shall heal my weakness; redeeming
   my life and crowning me with compassion, and filling my desire
   with good things: my youth shall be renewed like the eagle's. For
   we are saved by hope and we wait with patience for Your
   promises.
Let those who can hear Your voice speaking within them; I, relying
   upon Your inspired word, shall cry aloud: How great are Your
   words, O Lord! You have made all things in wisdom. Wisdom is
   "the Beginning": and it is in that Beginning that You made
   heaven and earth.

Augustine of Hippo; North Africa, 354–430

How God Answers the Soul

It is my nature that makes me love you often,
For I am love itself.

It is my longing that makes me love you intensely,
For I yearn to be loved from the heart.

It is my eternity that makes me love you long,
For I have no end.

Mechthild of Magdeburg. Germany. c. 1212–c. 1280

Unveiled Faces

And we, with unveiled faces
reflecting like mirrors
the glory of the Lord
grow brighter and brighter
as we are turned into
the image we reflect.

2 Corinthians 3:18

GIVE ME LIGHT

O God, give me light in my heart and light in my tongue and light
  in my hearing and light in my sight and light in my feeling and
  light in all my body and light before me and light behind me.
  Give me, I pray Thee, light on my right hand and light on my
  left hand and light above me and light beneath me, O Lord,
  increase light within me and give me light and illuminate me.

Ascribed to Muhammad; today's Saudi Arabia, c. 570-632

THAT YOU MAY ABOUND IN HOPE

And now may the God of hope
fill you with all joy and peace
in believing, that you may abound
in hope, through the power of
the Holy Spirit.

Romans 15:13

Concluding Prayer

MAY YOUR DAYS BE HAPPY

The winter will lose its cold, as the
    snow will be without whiteness,
The night without darkness, the
    heavens without stars, the day
    without light,
The flower will lose its beauty, all
    fountains their water, the sea its
    fish,
the tree its birds, the forest its
    beasts, the earth its harvest—
    All these will pass before anyone
    breaks the bonds of our love,
And before I cease caring for
    you in my heart.
May your days be happy in number
    as flakes of snow,
May your nights be peaceful, and
    may you be without troubles.

Matthew of Rievaulx; France,
twelfth to thirteenth century

Index
of Poem Titles

Special Acknowledgments

To Axel, my beloved, a heart overflowing with gratitude for all the research, energy, time, skills, ideas, support, and patient love you gave to me while this book was being birthed—and for the best years of my life.

To Tara: Thank you for shining your radiant spirit on me while I was working on this book, and always, and for the healing compassion you bring to the world.

To Matthew Fox, descendent of Jeremiah and Isaiah, for the blazing spirit and uncompromising courage with which you fight for justice on planet Earth.

To the faculty, administration, and staff of Princeton Theological Seminary, for an unsurpassable education in theology and spirituality.

To the faculty, administration, and staff of the University of Creation Spirituality, for the artistry, passion, knowledge, commitment, and hope you bring to our work at the bright blue table and everywhere.

To Tom Abel, for the earthiness and Trappist wisdom in the prayers you wrote for this book.

To Chris Batchelder, for your lovely prayer and Sufi spirit.

To Shirley Breese, for bringing as much creativity as competence to the task of inputting this manuscript, and for your enspirited friendliness on even the most pressured days.

To Tessa Bielecki, for your wonderful prayer, and for incarnating in our century the passionate spirit of Teresa of Avila.

To Mel Bricker, gracious and lovely pastor and poet, for the beautiful prayer you contributed to this book, and for your healing presence in the world.

To Sri Eknath Easwaran, for your deeply moving prayer, and for your ongoing example of the highest forms of love.

To Mary Franklin for your assistance in research, and for the untiring and loving warmth you contribute to the UCS community and to the world all around you.

To Judy Gaar, for the quiet depths you brought to Medieval Mystics and expressed in your prayer.

To Eryk Hanut, master of all the forms of love celebrated in this book, for the creative beauty in your prayer and in your soul.

To Andrew Harvey, for the beautiful prayers you translated for this book, for your huge soul; and for the love you inspire in my heart and in the world.

To William O. Harris of the Department of Archives and Special Collections, Princeton Theological Seminary, for your kind assistance with research.

To Mara Hawks, for the beauty and wisdom and depth in the prayers written for this book; and to Hilary, for inspiring so much love.

To William Haynes, physician who prays with his patients, for the love in your prayer, your heart, your practice, and your books.

To José Hobday, for the prayers from the magnificent Native American oral tradition that you consented to put in writing for this book, for your indomitable spirit, and for your example of consummate female strength.

To Sulekh Jain, for your kind help with research on the Jain faith.

To Frances Jones, who edited this book with a luminous mind and with so much graciousness: Thank you for all your ideas and creative help and for bringing to your work the highest gift of all, wisdom.

To Dr. Irfan Ahmad Khan, for your help with Islamic spirituality.

To Adelle Krauser, a superb copyeditor: Thank you for your extraordinary thoroughness and a truly outstanding contribution to this manuscript.

To Ling Lucas of the Nine Muses and Apollo Agency, for the warmth that sings in your voice on the telephone, and for the rare blend of refined professional abilities and spirituality that you have brought to our work together.

To Marguerite Manning, beloved friend and relative, for your help and your love.

To Mary-Theresa McCarthy, for the splendid French translations you wrote for this book, and for your friendship.

To Ronald Nakasone, for the gift of loveliness—in your prayer, and in your spirit.

To Margaret Payne, for both of your prayers, for the pleasure in our friendship, and for caring about urban spirituality.

To Thomas Renaud, for the power in your prayer and in your ministry.

To Robinton M. Rivetna, of the Federation of Zoroastrian Associations of North America, for so greatly aiding my research on Zoroastrianism.

To Jim Roberts, for all the earthy wisdom and vision in your prayer.

To Belvie Rooks, for the lovely prayer you wrote for this book, and for your example of grace in the world.

To Andrew Schelling, for your outstanding translations of Mirabai.

To Jon Martin Schwartz, contemporary mystic, for the riches in your prayer and your heart.

To David Steindl-Rast, for the contemplative beauty in your prayer and for all the prayers and love you have inspired in the world.

To Jeremy Taylor, for the unusual harmony of intellect and heart in your bright spirit and in the prayer you wrote for this book.

To Wayne Teasdale, Christian *sannyasi,* for your mystical prayer and for your huge contribution to East-West unity.

To Anita Wheatcroft, for the time, love, and giftedness you gave to this book.

To Michael Ziegler, rabbi without walls, for the contemplative spirit in your prayer and for your activism in society.